I.S.A.M. Monographs: Number 20

From Print to Plastic: Publishing and Promoting America's Popular Music (1900–1980)

RUSSELL SANJEK

Institute for Studies in American Music
Conservatory of Music
Brooklyn College
of the City University of New York

Published by the Institute for Studies in American Music
Conservatory of Music
Brooklyn College of the City University of New York
Brooklyn, New York 11210

FOREWORD

Russell Sanjek was Senior Research Fellow of the Institute for Studies in American Music in the spring of 1982. In addition to research and writing under the fellowship, he directed a semester-long seminar on "American Popular Music and Its Business." He also delivered the two public lectures that became the basis for the present monograph. The first, presented at Brooklyn College on 3 May, was called "Building the Marvelous Hit-Making Machine, 1900-1941." The second, read at the Graduate Center of the City University of New York on 10 May, was titled "Paying to Play and Playing for Pay, 1942-1980."

Russell Sanjek retired in the spring of 1981 from the post of Vice President for Public Relations of Broadcast Music, Inc.; he had been with BMI since its inception in 1940. Before that, in the 1930s, he had been editor of *HRS Society Rag*, one of the first serious jazz periodicals. He has been a member of the publications committee of the American Composers Alliance, the President's Music Committee of the People-to-People Program, and the New York State Council on the Arts. He was the first director of the BMI-sponsored Student Composers Awards program, has served as chairman of the Jazz and Folk Music Advisory Committee for Lincoln Center for the Performing Arts in New York City, and as a member of the Jazz Committee of the National Endowment for the Arts, not to mention the Hall of Fame Advisory Committee of the Country Music Association and other councils, committees, boards, and support organizations—almost all related to American popular music and its business.

Mr. Sanjek is at work on a large long-range history for Oxford University Press; its working title is *American Popular Music and Its Business: The First 400 Years.*

H. Wiley Hitchcock, Director
Institute for Studies in American Music
February 1983

CONTENTS

BUILDING THE MARVELOUS
HIT-MAKING MACHINE: 1900-1941

The Music Publishing Business Before 1900

The men who began to print and disseminate popular songs in New York City after 1885, later settling along Tin Pan Alley (between Fifth and Sixth Avenues on 28th Street), did not invent the business but they did introduce mass production and promotion of American popular songs. Perhaps their most important contribution to the economic development of song publishing was the "marvelous hit-making machine," which with its flaws and excesses functioned for decades until the publishers of music on plastic—the recording companies—appropriated it for the exploitation of *their* mass-produced products.

There are many interesting parallels between the development of American book and music publishing, whose history began in England. Once Gutenberg had perfected printing to produce the artificial handwriting which was to replace the English Stationers' Guild's laboriously executed "manu-scripts," mass reproduction of the printed word began. Music printing lagged behind, however, until improved music type and engraving permitted reasonably accurate duplication of its far more demanding notated language.

Relying on property rights to their work granted first by Henry VIII in the early 1520s— the exclusive "privilege" to duplicate the product or, in effect, to exercise the "right to copy" or to hold "copy right"—merchant stationers-turned-printers also began publication of popular songs, vocal and instrumental art music, and the musical psalters whose purchase and use in worship were required by the Tudor heads of state. Publication of the common man's music, the broadside street ballads that were hawked through town and country for a penny each, was usually left to those printers who were allowed by law and the rules of the Stationers' Company to print "on one side only" of a piece of paper. For many years both books and printed music, which are not essential consumer items, were offered in a marketplace that determined its own dimensions, and little effort was made by either trade to extend those dimensions.

The Puritan Commonwealth's repression of most popular culture notwithstanding, in 1650 John Playford began to print and distribute popular vocal and dance music from a store in London, a century before any similar enterprise was formed on the European continent. Around 1695 Thomas Cross, Jr. invented sheet music much as we know it today when he used pewter instead of expensive copperplate as the medium on which to engrave or punch the words and music of songs from the London royal opera and playhouses.

In the absence of legal or economic restraints, price-fixing, anti-competitive, copyright-owning monopolies came into being in the early eighteenth century. Like the conger eel, for which these bookseller combinations were named, they devoured all within their reach, including writers, poets, composers, and songwriters. Dealing only with each other (at mutually favorable rates) and controlling retail sales, "congers" of bookseller-publishers dominated their world for decades. With a product that was sold principally "on demand," they found little need for either an efficient distribution system or any exploitation, as we know it today, of their publications. The bookseller monopolies were destroyed after a long battle in the English courts, before Parliament and the House of Lords, which finally affirmed copyright as an authors' privilege late in the eighteenth century.

The sale of printed music, musical instruments, and supplies had become profitable bus-iness by the time of the American Revolution, and a number of successful British publishers opened elegant shops in London and other major cities. It was from these that many upper-class colonists ordered the latest sheet music and collections of theater and instrumental music to be shipped across the Atlantic. Our first professional songwriter and music publisher, William Billings of Boston, learned much of his craft from imported tracts on composition, as did others of his fellow tunebook compilers and singing masters.

The original American copyright act, which became law in 1790, was framed, in the words of the Constitution, to "promote the progress of science and useful arts, by securing for limited times, to authors and inventors, the exclusive rights to their respective writings." This legislation, based on the already archaic English law (the 1709 "Statute of Queen Anne"), was a "narrow, stingy law that had to be expanded piecemeal during the century that followed."[1] Composers and songwriters were the last to benefit from the bit-by-bit expansion of its protection: music was first mentioned only in the 1831 revision.

The emigrant English and European musicians and composers who opened the original American music-publishing houses in the Federal era had learned how to engrave music, and the first printed pieces they offered for sale were made by this process. Engraving permitted notation to be easily corrected; works of elegant clarity were possible, as were attractive illustrations; and the finished result was more accurate than music published from movable type. Music plates were easy to store and could be taken down from the shelves whenever demand warranted. As these plates piled up in storerooms over the years, early nineteenth-century American music publisher-merchants became increasingly hesitant to take risks on new music by their countrymen, music that had come to be considered inferior to foreign compositions. They relied instead on a profitable body of imported music that could be reproduced in the United States at an even lower cost than in Europe. It was copyright-free music, to be had for the taking because of a biased provision in the original law denying protection of any kind to non-American printed materials. Only one-tenth of all music printed in the United States during the first quarter of the nineteenth century was by Americans. Even as late as the early 1900s, 70% of all piano rolls and recordings were of foreign music.[2]

The fewer than one dozen pre-Civil War American firms which printed most of all published sheet music concentrated on foreign vocal and instrumental music. Theirs was chiefly a mail-order business, and the trade's best customers were music teachers throughout the country, who purchased half of all music printed, at a 50% discount, for resale to their pupils.

Only the most productive popular-music writers received any royalties from the sale of their sheet music throughout the nineteenth century. Stephen Foster's contracts during the 1850s called for 10% of the retail price of all music sold after production costs had been recouped. The sale of more than 100,000 copies of his most successful song, *Old Folks at Home*, during the 1850s, to a native population of about 28 million, was equivalent to a sale of more than one million copies today. Two decades later, William Shakespeare Hays, the most successful songwriter in the immediate post-Civil War period, received 2½ cents per copy printed regardless of price (which varied from 25 to 60 cents). America's potential market for hit songs had grown in twenty years from the one in about 250 persons who purchased copies of the Foster song to the one in 150 who bought Hays's *We Parted by the River*, which had sales in excess of 300,000 copies. Those writers less well-known than Foster and Hays were not as fortunate in the matter of royalties: they turned over their songs to music firms for $5 to $10, a meal, or on occasion a bottle of whiskey.

American music publishers first emulated monopolistic book-publishing practices in 1855, when they formed the Board of Music Trade of the United States. This association of 25 music houses came into being in response to a declaration of war against their most important source of income, the sale of copyright-free music, the price of which had been fixed industry-wide by unwritten general consent. One major New York publisher, William Hall, had announced a price reduction by 50% at retail of his entire stock, using an open letter in both the music-trade and the general press to convey the news. Peace was hastily arranged following the creation of the Board of Music Trade, which included all major music publishers, even the rebel Hall. As the established book trade was doing, the Board adopted a "courtesy of the trade" policy in dealing with foreign works, assigning exclusive rights to individual publishers in the music of the European composers whose work was most in demand.

Within the next fifteen years a few members of the Board acquired control of virtually all American popular music printed since the creation of the Republic, thanks to either the death or the dire economic straits of the original copyright holders. Gradually all power was concentrated in the hands of these houses, most newcomers being barred from admission to the Board of Music Trade. As a classic "trust," it continued to restrain trade by fixing and sustaining a uniform standard price for all music, effectively destroying all competition in many ways.

The major problem in the last decades of the century to face the Board, whose name was changed in 1895 to the Music Publishers Association, was the surreptitious reprinting of the members' best-selling sheet music by pirates working out of Canada, who then sold the music at one-sixth of retail price. Eventually joint regulations imposed by the American and Canadian governments in response to strenuous Association efforts put a temporary end to such counterfeited music. However, as the market for printed music continued to expand, illegal printers again began to harass the trade, posing a problem that has continued, in one form or another, to the present.

In the 1890s, the largest music publishing house in America, Oliver Ditson of Boston, whose founder had been instrumental in forming the Board of Music Trade, noted in a handsome commemorative brochure[3] that the firm owned the plates, catalogue, and good will of more than fifty firms. The Ditson firm stocked "seven miles of printed music and music books," as well as pianos, organs, other instruments, and music supplies. The house maintained one of the "most liberal advertising departments in the trade," keeping in touch with customers through advertisements in leading music papers. It also regularly mailed "little booklets and thematic lists telling of new publications [to] more than 30,000 musical people living in the United States and Canada." The most profitable and prestigious music house in America, Ditson's had become chiefly a wholesaler, supplying 2,000 music dealers throughout the country, who found it "easier to send their combined orders to a wholesale house with such magnificent resources, and where promptness and dispatch are the watchwords, than to send to a large number of small publishers for a few copies of each piece."[4]

The established music trade's best customers no longer were chiefly music teachers, as they had been until after the Civil War, but a growing number of newly rich Americans, products of an expanding economy, and the "cultured classes," who bought sheet music from piano teachers to be played and sung by their daughters in the family parlor. The majority of printed music sold was non-copyright European music and such American "popular-music" favorites as the waltz-song and quartet-song. The leading publishers had little interest in the "cheap music" whose use was growing in concert saloons, wine rooms, the "free-and-easies," dance halls, beer gardens, early vaudeville theaters, and other places where vernacular music prevailed. Most stage performers and minstrel show vocalists were pleased to feature the songs issued by the established firms in return for having their pictures printed on sheet-music covers.

For example, William A. Pond & Co., publisher of most New York theater music prior to 1890, bought David Braham and Edward "Ned" Harrigan's first "Mulligan Guard" song outright for $50. Harrigan wanted printed music with which to promote himself and his new stage piece, the first of many successful comic farces with songs that paved the way for vaudeville and the American musical comedy. In obliging him, Pond & Co. came into control of more than one hundred Harrigan and Braham songs that followed. During the years when Pond & Co. sat back, doing nothing to exploit and promote this music, Harrigan and his stage partner Tony Hart performed it nightly for several generations of theater-goers, providing the publisher with songs that became internationally popular and highly profitable. This practice was universal in the pre-Tin Pan Alley music business, which depended almost exclusively on the leading entertainers, whose pictures graced the elaborately printed covers, to create demand and sales by singing its "popular music." While the newest art music was usually mailed gratis to important musical artists as well as to the trade press for review, vaudeville and variety performers wishing to use the old-line music houses' songs were charged retail prices for them. Some of the major publishers did issue monthly magazines containing printed new music, but these were little more than house-organ catalogues generally devoted to "classical and romantic finer" music.

The establishment of reciprocal international copyright, enacted in 1891, ended American access to new foreign music—at least, without regard to copyright—but most of the major firms were able to maintain control in the United States of the Old World's "superior music" through arrangements with British and European houses. Only a publisher with substantial financial assets, however, could enter into such an affiliation. Left to their own devices and ingenuity, the founders of new small publishing houses interested chiefly in American popular songs resorted to the use of advertising, sales, and promotion methods that had been developed by American big business. Markets yet unperceived awaited them, soon to be created by the growth of a player-piano industry and by another machine designed to reproduce music mechanically, Thomas Edison's phonograph.

Much as would the post-World War II music houses when faced with the annoying presence of hillbilly and race music, the established art- and parlor-music publishers failed to perceive the future. It was in the hands of music publishers specializing in new popular American music—first formed around 1885, whose founders—the Witmark Brothers, Edward B. Marks and Joseph Stern, Maurice Shapiro, Leo Feist, songwriter Harry von Tilzer, Will Rossiter of Chicago, F. A. Mills, Joe Jordan of Philadelphia, the Detroit businessman and dairy owner Jerome Remick, and others—were, as one of them, Isidore Witmark, remembered, youngsters who had caught on and had a fair notion of the direction in which they were headed. What they knew least about was music and words, what they cared about least might be answered by the same phrase. They discovered that there was money in popular song.[5]

Witmark and the other publishers had already been exposed to the spirit of go-getting salesmanship abroad in the land—a new kind of merchandising expounded by John Henry Patterson, the genius of the American Cash Register Company. Patterson looked for sales-men who could be taught to sell, rather than relying only on those who were born with the gift, and he emphasized that familiarity with the product to be pushed must be inculcated in the public. The Tin Pan Alley men taught their salesmen the art of publicizing a song by constant repetition, or "songplugging," and they began to sell popular music.

The New Century and Popular-Song Publishing

With sheet music selling from 25 to 60 cents a copy, the wholesale value of manufactured printed music reported to the government more than tripled between 1890 and 1909, rising from $1.7 million to $5.5 million. In 1909 over 27 million phonograph records and cylinders were manufactured (with a wholesale value of nearly $12 million), and more than 25,000 songs were entered for copyright,[6] a new historical peak complementing the parallel growth of piano sales to the still all-time high of 365,000 units.[7] Twenty years earlier the Music Teachers National Association had announced that half a million pre-adults were getting keyboard instruction from its members. Now their pupils had grown up, and with them were uncounted hundreds of thousands who had also learned to play the instrument. And, of course, anybody could "play" the Pianola with its paper music-rolls, or the phonograph.

The first harbinger of things to come from new technology affecting music appeared a few years after the Civil War: a reed organ operated by a perforated paper music-roll. The auto-matic music industry that followed grew slowly until the late 1890s. In 1902 the Aeolian Company, having purchased many patents and having refinanced its operations with a capi-talization of $15 million (more than the amount invested by the entire American piano and organ industry in 1890), launched the pedal-operated player piano known as the Pianola with a dramatic advertising and public-relations campaign. A single factor, however, threatened the company's determination to control the business: failure by either the courts or the Congress to resolve the issue of whether or not any mechanical reproduction of music, such as a piano roll or a phonograph recording, was an infringement of the copyright laws. Having already built a catalogue of more than 8,000 selections, and adding 3,000 more each year, Aeolian intended to maintain its lead over the competition and entered into secret agreements with most members of the Music Publishers Association. These contracts gave Aeolian exclusive rights to draw upon the catalogues of participating music firms for a period of 35 years, with a royalty of 10% to be paid whenever the issue of infringement was resolved in the copyright owners' favor. Aeolian also agreed to pay all costs in a legal action that would be taken up to the Supreme Court. That body was expected to make new law, in effect, by affirming the right of both parties to enter into such an arrangement.

Although the courts subsequently ruled against the copyright owners, competing piano-roll manufacturers and representatives of the young phonograph industry cried "Monopoly!" when they learned of the secret arrangement. In the atmosphere of national trust-busting then prevalent, Congress and the President were roused to action, and a compulsory licensing provision was added to the Copyright Act of 1909. For the first time in American history, the peacetime bargaining process between a supplier and a user was regulated by the federal government, and the price for use of private property fixed by national law. A royalty of 2 cents for each piano roll, phonograph record, or cylinder manufactured was to be paid to the copyright owner. In addition, seeking to guard against any future copyright monopoly on the order of that which Aeolian and the Music Publishers Association had intended to form, the law provided that, once permission was granted for the mechanical reproduction of a piece of music, the piece was available for the same fee to any others who chose to use it.

Aeolian, the prime mover in an effort to create a monopoly of mechanically reproduced music, benefited from the legislation it had inspired. Rather than pay a 10% royalty for the music it used, a fee of only 2 cents for each composition was required. The company continued to dominate the player-piano business with a major share of the sales, which grew from 45,414 units in 1909 to the peak year of 1923, when 205,556 instruments were sold (a major portion of the $59 million in total piano sales).

The compulsory licensing requirement was punishment visited alike not only on the 87 old-line publishers, with 381,589 compositions, who had been party to the Aeolian plan but on 117 other music firms, controlling 503,597 compositions, who had not.[8] Among the latter were many Tin Pan Alley houses, newcomers to the business who had brought to it new promotional techniques that were raising sales figures and profits to new heights, chiefly because of the songplugging they pioneered.

Although stage performers had always been important in building public appetite for new music, the established music business had neglected to make use of that power. But the new music-men did not; they turned to the vaudeville artists to help create demand for their merchandise. Jay Witmark and his brothers were the first to give away "artists' copies" of new music, printed on the cheapest paper and without any cover illustrations. The

Witmarks also began to print a line of popular-song arrangements in various keys for distribution to bandleaders weeks before the songs went on retail sale. For the first time in their history, music publishers employed traveling salesmen, sending them out on the road to contact music jobbers, the recently risen middlemen who bought at a 50% discount and sold to retailers after an appropriate markup.

Tin Pan Alley publishers also recognized the potential of the phonograph record as a promotional aid during the record industry's formative years, and they regularly sent notices of new music to the record manufacturers. Discs and cylinders of new songs were purchased from the record companies to be placed in coin-operated music-playing machines in New York City and other places where music was recorded; these were forerunners of the jukebox. The publishers also wrote to the popular artists, who generally chose the music they recorded, and even sent representatives to contact them before each session.

In 1904 Enrico Caruso was signed as the first exclusive recording artist of the Victor Talking Machine Company, which soon was to be the largest American recording firm.[9] The Italian tenor received $4,000 for recording ten sides and an annual retainer of $2,000 for the next five years; before he died in 1921, he had earned $2 million in royalties.

Caruso was one of the few operatic singers of his time with a seemingly innate sense of how to make recordings (where to stand, when to move back and forth, and other physical adjustments required by the acoustic recording process). There was also a small group of popular singers who had mastered recording techniques, principally the ability to fit a complete song onto the two-minute record side of the time. As free-lance performers they went from company to company, recording the same songs with the same arrangements. The art and social music trade's general disdain for popular music was reflected in the price structure for recordings of this period. Caruso's discs sold for $2 when he was the soloist, but increased, in dollar increments, depending on the number of operatic singers who sang with him. The number of performers recording a popular song, however, did not affect the price; their work sold for 35 cents a copy and they shared around $20 for each master record they made.

Tin Pan Alley's hit-making apparatus was fully operative when the twentieth century opened, in a pattern that obtained for decades, with variations dictated only by changing technology. Its function was to stimulate live performances, in as great a number as possible, to attract sheet-music buyers. The process began with orders for a few thousand "artists' copies" of a song, to be distributed by the publisher and his songpluggers to performers and musicians. If a favorable public response followed, the Tin Pan Alley men ordered an edition of 10,000 "regular" copies on heavier paper for the retail trade. This version featured the lithographed portrait of the popular artist who had agreed to push the song on an exclusive basis in return for a gift, as well as a royalty on each piece sold. Five hundred dollars' worth of advertising, with the performer's picture featured and his enthusiasm for the new piece quoted, was dispatched to a major entertainment trade journal, with a written account of how successful the artist's interpretation had been. The space was contracted for on an annual basis, with the tacit understanding that the advertiser's music would receive favorable mention. This initial promotion campaign involved the outlay of about $1,300, a gamble expected to result in one out of every hundred new pieces at least repaying its original investment.

Once orders for regular copies of a piece indicated potential success, new editions were rushed into print. Now the songpluggers concentrated on the piece, obtaining every performance possible, in any venue, at any cost, and by every physical and mechanical contrivance available, until public demand slacked off; then another song was selected as a new candidate for the hit-making machine's attention.

As more publishing firms went into business and more songpluggers were involved in the process, the production of new songs increased, but the shelf-life of a hit grew shorter. In the 1890s it had been two to three years; by the First World War it had fallen to less than one.

Success was not without cost. Aware of the importance of their contribution to the music industry's growing prosperity, stage and vaudeville artists raised the price for their cooperation; those initial shares of sheet-music royalties, together with small gifts, were replaced by subsidization of stage costumes and theatrical scenery, and finally by hard cash only, in a cycle that evolved in little more than a decade. Hundreds of thousands of dollars went into performers' pockets each year, a practice certainly known to theater managers at whose box offices the publishers' checks were usually cashed. By 1915 more than a half-million dollars was being paid annually to vaudeville performers alone for song-boosting, and publishers were at each others' throats for control of paid performances.

It was action by the top management of the powerful Keith-Orpheum vaudeville circuit that brought about the establishment in 1917 of the Music Publishers Protective Association (MPPA), to replace the publishers' group that had collapsed after the Aeolian debacle. The new Association had a single mission, one imposed on it by the head of the Keith-Orpheum circuit: to stamp out vaudeville's "payment system." Veteran music publisher Louis Bernstein reminisced in 1956 about the day the Tin Pan Alley publishers were summoned to the impresario's office:

. . . he told us, "I want subsidy of our acts stopped by 12 noon tomorrow and I want all you top publishers to meet me in my office and give me your pledge to that effect. Otherwise, our 187 theatres will bar out all [your] songs and material." By gosh we were all there and it stopped. At least for a time. . . . So what happened? My firm cut in Al Jolson on some 40 to 50 songs. . . . I cut in Jolson plenty. At that time we had exclusive contracts to the Winter Garden songs, and Jolson was best "influenced" by getting a piece of a song, a by-line as co-author and his name and photo on the title page. The last we would have done anyway because it was a plus to put some headliner's picture on a song sheet, reading "As featured by Nora Bayes at the Palace" or "Eddie Cantor at the Ziegfeld Follies."[10]

MPPA's Articles of Agreement included one clause banning any advertising that featured artists who promoted new songs. It was almost immediately ignored, as were other more significant sections of the new code of practices, and within a year a leading member was hailed before his peers and charged with flagrant abuses. His defense was this: "What assurance have we that our competition will do likewise? They probably never will, and if we lay off they'll have that much greater advantage."[11] The "gratuity system" continued and in fact went into high gear.

The American parlor piano had always been the domain of women, and with the growing exploitation of popular song sheet music they became its chief consumer. In the late 1890s major department stores, whose clientele was chiefly female, opened sheet music departments, complete with demonstrators, where the newest hit songs were sold in vast numbers. The energetic R. H. Macy & Co. of New York was an important outlet for this business, and when it engaged in price wars with competitors tremendous quantities of printed popular songs were disposed of at bargain prices which occasionally fell to a few cents a copy. The standard price of music fell to 10 cents in 1915, and the dime stores, principally F. W. Woolworth's 1,200-odd 5 & 10 Cent Stores became a favorite source of supply around the country and even abroad.[12] Usually women pianists demonstrated the new songs at counters there (purposely located at the rear of the shop in order to manipulate the flow of traffic), selling some 200 million copies of music in a single year.[13]

Low-price sheet-music sales continued to rise dramatically, peaking in 1918 with *Till We Meet Again*, by Ray Egan and Richard Whiting, which sold 3.5 million copies in a few months. However, rising production costs made it impossible to produce ten-cent sheet music without a loss, and many believed that a post-World War I recession would bring about a serious collapse of the music business.

Records, Radio, and the Music Business: 1920-1930

Million-copy sales of sheet music came to an end in 1920, following a 50% increase in production costs as a result of a printers' strike and a concurrent paper shortage. Prices rose to 30 cents a piece, driving the Woolworth chain out of the music business. Almost overnight, in 1921 the American public turned from sheet-songs to phonograph records for its music. The first song to be made popular entirely by record-machine exploitation had been *Mary* in 1919, written by George Stoddard. It had been turned down by every New York publisher, even though the writer wanted only $100 for all rights; but then a recording of it sold 300,000 copies in three months and Victor eventually paid Stoddard $15,000 in mechanical royalties. The following year Paul Whiteman came up with a two-sided record hit that sold 2 million copies, *Whispering* and *The Japanese Sandman*, songs Whiteman had personally selected to record. The bandleader was promptly signed by Leo Feist, Inc., as a "staff writer" at $10,000 a year. With his control of 11 bands in New York and 17 on the road, plus 40 others that played Whiteman arrangements, the bandleader was a major source of exploitation. Eddie Cantor was the first popular vocalist to join the august ranks of Caruso and other superstar operatic singers: he made a five-year exclusive deal in 1920 with Emerson, which promised him $220,000; but when the company overextended its credit, the Follies star moved to the Columbia label and made even more.

The big money was going to performers and music publishers, not to songwriters, unless they chanced to own the music firm that printed their music—as did, for example, Irving Berlin. He had been the country's best-known and most popular writer ever since his great hit *Alexander's Ragtime Band* had come out (in 1911), and his songs went unscathed during the ten-cent sheet-music crisis, maintaining a 30-cent price, reflecting his prestige. During the war, Berlin realized almost $160,000 annually in royalties alone. By 1922, it became apparent to this wise music-man, who had the opportunity to study his firm's financial accounts since he was the senior partner in the enterprise, that record sales were outpacing those of sheet music. Berlin's *Say It With Music* sold 375,000 printed copies in a 75-week period—but more than 1 million records and 100,000 piano rolls. Most songwriters, not being in so fortunate a position, had no idea of the sales of their music and received little or no share in sales income and royalties. Nor did they or the music industry itself receive any money for performance of their material on the new-fangled radio.

Almost from the start of commercial broadcasting, radio's potential as a new promotional medium for popular music was self-evident. Publishers in the cities with new radio stations immediately went to work to win the friendship of radio performers. Beginning in 1922, when the number of active stations jumped from 28 in January to 570 in December and broadcasters (who were essentially technicians at the time) attempted to cope with programming, the major houses sent their songpluggers to "assist" the new industry with subsidized musical entertainment. Certain songpluggers became well-known air personalities, and teams of exploitation men toured the country's stations, singing and pushing new songs. Soon, more than 100 hotels from coast to coast had installed "remote" broadcast facilities, over which dance orchestras (often formed with financial backing from music publishers) played the latest songs.

The introduction of network broadcasting in 1926 brought ever-growing audiences, attracted by free entertainment, and consequently led to the hunt on commercially sponsored variety and musical programs for that publicizing of a song by constant repetition which produced hits. Even as the industry inveighed against the concentrated air play that resulted, charging that it reduced the very life of songs (hence royalties), *Variety* noted (10 April 1929, p. 56) that "it is doubtful whether in any other field there is so much chicanery, double-crossing, double-dealing, duplicity, and hooey, a condition that comes about not so much because of economic jealousy but because of the petty business of 'landing a plug.'"

MPPA's responsibility to fight the "playing for pay" that had now become a major problem in broadcasting music over the radio waves was being shared by the American Society of Composers, Authors, and Publishers (ASCAP), custodian of the right to license public performance for profit in virtually all popular music of the time. While the Society struggled to curb subsidization of radio performers, its publisher members continued to engage in that "petty business."

The revised Copyright Act of 1909 had included a provision governing public performance for profit, but until ASCAP was formed in 1914 the issue of its application to popular music was never tested. The majority decision written by Chief Justice Oliver Wendell Holmes in the landmark case in 1916, *Victor Herbert vs. Shanley's Restaurant* (the latter an expensive New York restaurant where live pre-Muzak was performed), had affirmed the Society's right to require payment for the use of its music and continued to serve as the cornerstone for all the organization's licensing efforts:

> . . . The defendant's performances [of ASCAP music] are not eleemosynary. They are part of a total for which the public pays, and the fact that the price of the whole is attributed to a particular item which those present are expected to order is not important. It is true that the music is not the sole object, but neither is the food, which probably could be got cheaper elsewhere. The object is a repast in surroundings that to people having limited powers of conversation or disliking the rival noise give a luxurious pleasure not to be had from eating a silent meal. If music did not pay, it would be given up. If it pays, it pays out of the public's pocket. Whether it pays or not the purpose of employing it is for profit, and that is enough. [15]

As had the American Hotel Association, the American Federation of Musicians, the Motion Picture Exhibitors, and every other body before them whose constituents fell within the purview of the 1909 Copyright Act's public-performance section, American broadcasters protested immediately when it was suggested in 1922 by ASCAP that they too pay to play its music. Their argument against doing so ran along lines that had been laid down by other, earlier, reluctant music-users: because we play your music we make it popular, and therefore you songwriters and music publishers should be grateful for this advertising and ought to look somewhere else for license fees!

Perhaps because publisher members of ASCAP were reluctant to disturb their relations with broadcasters and urged caution, hoping to preserve their use of the medium as a promotional tool, the Society's first collections from radio in 1925 of $58,478.05 represented under 10% of its total income that year. But the figure grew slowly, and in 1929 radio license fees were $619,398.94, almost 35% of a total income of $1,777,288.08.

Most Tin Pan Alley publishing houses had been reluctant to support the Society in its early days; just after World War I only six firms, almost all dealing in "production" or theater music, had joined. Not until late 1920, when there was a prospect of sharing in an initial $250,000 collected from music users, did the holdout firms begin to join. The price for their affiliation was surrender of the traditional European performing-right-society distribution policy which ASCAP had first embraced: the distribution of two-thirds of all income (after expenses) to authors and composers, and one-third to the publishers. In order to increase the Society's repertory by the addition of publishers' catalogues, the ASCAP songwriters agreed in 1920 to equal distribution of collections and equal makeup of the board.

Despite this pragmatic show of unity, relations between songwriters and publishers did not improve perceptibly during the Twenties. The creators of popular music continued to have reason for complaint about their treatment by the music houses, which had changed little in more than a century. Songs were still usually purchased outright. The distribution of mechanical and sheet-music royalties was inequitable or even non-existent; the publisher who gave even the smallest share of royalty income to a writer was labeled a "radical" or "liberal." There were as many forms of contract as there were music publishers, and few of either were fair to those who wrote the words and music. Publishers cited business conditions as a reason for their conduct. Due to the tripling of sheet-music production costs in 1920, the number of copies sold declined seriously throughout the decade, for a gross that never rose above $15 million annually. Because of the public's growing acceptance of radio, record sales had also slipped, from $105 million in 1921 to $46 million in 1930 (but the publishers continued to receive an average of $2 million annually in mechanical royalties). In 1930 ASCAP's total income was slightly under $2 million, of which radio paid $812,296.50.

The brightest spot for a small group of songwriters and their publishers was Broadway, where music houses working with theatrical producers (who extracted their pounds of flesh for the privilege) built great standard catalogues of sophisticated musical-comedy songs that were several cuts above routine popular music. Music publishers had been reluctant to subsidize some production costs but cooperated in order to acquire the copyrights of the 611 musicals offered on Broadway during the 1920s, of which only one of three was a financial success. Plugged to popularity by their use in long-running shows in New York and on the road, songs by the Gershwins, Jerome Kern, Cole Porter, Vincent Youmans, Rudolf Friml, Sigmund Romberg, and other show-tune composers were now the music business's most important money-makers. Production writers had become the new aristocrats of Tin Pan Alley: Romberg, for example, grossed over $1.5 million from the Broadway productions alone of his *The Student Prince*, *Blossom Time*, and *The Desert Song.*

When the talking-picture makers learned that popular music attracted people into movie houses to a far larger extent than the silent-picture "theme songs," a grand exodus of the most productive songwriters followed as the motion-picture industry literally bought up Tin Pan Alley and moved it to the Coast. MGM bought 51% of Robbins Music and later added Leo Feist and Miller Music; the Warner Brothers acquired six major houses for over a million dollars and incorporated them into the Music Publishers Holding Corporation; Paramount Pictures created its own holding company, Famous Music; and lesser film makers acquired their own music publishing companies and promotion outlets. In all, 320 song-writers and composers were working on sound-picture lots in the summer of 1929. Until the Depression hit the movie industry several years later, these New Yorkers transplanted to the land of perpetual sunshine and a 9:00-5:00 office routine enjoyed a social and eco-nomic status most of them had never known. Any argument with publishers over sheet-music and recording royalties seemed trivial in the face of a guaranteed $12,000 to $35,000 annual income on the average, with as much as $1,000 weekly to the best-known. It was the largest income from music that many songwriters had ever enjoyed, and life was good while it lasted. It spoiled them, however, as the publishers would soon learn.

Popular Music in the Troubled Thirties

Efforts to form an independent songwriters' body along the lines of the Music Publishers Protective Association were frustrated before the Songwriters Protective Association (SPA) became a tenuous reality in 1931. That year, with the support of leading writers and com-posers, many with Broadway and Hollywood experience, a "Standard Uniform Popular Songwriters Contract" was framed, and it won the approval of both ASCAP and the MPPA. In it were established for the first time for songwriters a minimum royalty of 33-1/3% of income from sheet-music and record sales, 2½ cents per copy of sheet sales, regular accounting periods, the right to inspect all financial records of publishers, arbitration of disputes, and other gains. But only a few publishers adopted the SPA agreement, in spite of MPPA's support of it. The majority who refused maintained that any organization of songwriters would put them out of business. Undeterred, members of the new organization continued their uphill fight for recognition of the SPA contract and the rights it guaranteed.

The "presumptuous" demands of those who created its product were only part of many problems confronting the music business when the great Depression of the 1930s became a fact of life. Sheet-music sales were down: only the most successful songs now sold as many as 200,000 copies. Sales of phonograph records fell, too, to the twentieth-century low of $5.6 million in 1933, and mechanical royalties from them, which a small group of songwriters now shared for the first time, plummeted. It was ASCAP income, chiefly, that helped to sustain many songwriter and publisher members during this gloomy period. In 1932, Irving Berlin, George Gershwin, Vincent Youmans, and 49 other truly creative writers each got from the Society only $1,000 more than singer Al Jolson[16]—a "playing for pay" inequity that was a reminder of the old "gratuity" practices.

American network radio had become the chief purveyor of popular music. In one week in 1938, as sampled by the Federal Communications Commission, 51.6% of all programming, both sponsored and sustaining (or without advertising), included popular and light music, and the variety programs that depended on both. Of 6,000 hours of live programs, the networks and their affiliates devoted 2,291 hours to popular music and variety, and only 325 hours to the full range of news programs, sports, flashes, news, crop, and weather reports.[17]

The influence of songplugging on network music programming was revealed most dramatically in a study of ASCAP performance records for the year 1938 made by the National Association of Broadcasters (*Let's Stick to the Record*, published in 1940). A total of 388 songs, performed more than 10,000 times, accounted for 47.1% of all performances. An additional 2,121 selections accounted for 36.6% of all performances. Together, these 2,509 songs got more than 15 million network performances during 1938.

Because the business depended on hit songs, and because air play made songs hits, the pursuit of plugs and performances on radio became paramount. "Cutting-in" orchestra leaders and network radio stars as co-writers (as Jolson was for years) was so open that ASCAP called its members' attention to the New York State laws on commercial bribery. Unable to restrain its own members, the Music Publishers Protective Association called on the Federal Trade Commission, which drew up a code that was honored, however, more in the breach than otherwise. Songpluggers organized themselves into a union that was eventually recognized by the American Federation of Labor, but its function was to combat play-for-pay rather than to secure fair wages and proper working conditions for its members. The evil continued. The caretakers of the hit-making machine had become its servitors, and the bribery and malpractice prevalent for years was officially christened "payola" by *Variety* on 19 October 1938.

During the late 1930s three recapitulations of performances secured by the hit-making machine were published weekly. In two of these, appearing in *Variety* and *Billboard*, the hits were tabulated in alphabetical order. The third—the most widely recognized one, known as "the sheet"—was printed in Sunday editions of the *Enquirer*, a New York newspaper and racing form. In it, listed in numerical order of performances obtained, each week's songs were cited in a column garlanded with colorful racetrack jargon, detailing "the action" on three network-owned local stations (WABC, WEAF, and WJZ) from 5:00 p.m. to 1:00 a.m. on weekdays and all day on Sunday.

This information was generally unknown outside the radio and music business, but the more than half of all adult Americans who regularly tuned in to *Your Hit Parade* on Saturday night were offered much the same fare as that appearing on "the sheet." The program's usual claim—of offering the ten most "popular" songs of the previous week "as shown by a nation-wide survey"—was based in great part on information similar to that of "the sheet" and allied listings. The *Hit Parade*'s survey embraced performances on the air, sheet music sales, reports of requests to bandleaders and sales of their recordings, and use in jukeboxes—each category receiving equal value.

Music publishers, distrusting the sponsoring tobacco company's surveys, and knowing too well how easily the listings could be manipulated, suggested that only on-the-air performances and their own reports of sheet-music sales be taken into account. What concerned the music-men was the effect that the *Hit Parade*'s shifting ratings of each song had on sheet-music dealers, many of whom calculated their orders and returns by the rankings of the tunes on the program's countdown (or countup), from the tenth most popular song to the "Number One Song in All America."

Songpluggers were also disturbed by the effect of the tabulations on *their* work and asked that the method be revised so as to eliminate the intense competition for the top rankings at the end of each week. They suggested that

> . . . the value of a plug be taken into consideration, that one on a network radio show was worth more than one by a vocalist on a sustaining program. Publishers argued that there was no reason to eliminate the stress of competition, or making it any easier for firms that specialized in scores from films and legit productions . . . [who] would have a huge advantage over publishers who have to depend on free-lance writers for material.[18]

The fact was, however, that no matter how producers of *Your Hit Parade* arrived at the songs programmed as the ten best in America each week, the life of the songs on the program paralleled their progress and demise on "the sheet," which reported only the results of songplugging activities.

The Marvelous Hit-Making Machine at Work: 1939

Financed by Tin Pan Alley at the rate of $150,000 each week, the hit-making exploitation apparatus thrived on the general assumption that songs became hits because of their "spontaneous free-will acceptance by the public because of the inherent merit of the number."[19] But out of some 40 popular-music publishers in New York in 1939, only 13 of them, all affiliated in some way with the motion-picture business, dominated the top songs each week. Eight of these were owned outright, having been purchased from their original founders when the talking-picture makers, sensing the potential of popular music for box-office success, moved the best songwriters en masse to Hollywood. The move yielded unexpected dividends, for the successful exploitation of a motion picture's theme song or featured music usually added at least $1 million to its total gross, and general weekly expenditures of $5,000 to $15,000 for the purpose were well worth the risk. There was an additional financial return as well: the 13 motion-picture-connected firms collected two-thirds of the $2.5 million distributed to publishers by ASCAP in 1939 out of the Society's income of $6 million, the majority of this reflecting radio performances of music written for films.

Because they were regarded by publishers as "not commercial," most songs written by well-known composers for Hollywood musicals or Broadway shows were published only in "artists' copy" editions. Expecting them to be exploited by their publishers, the major labels recorded many of these, only to learn that few were promoted in any way. Only if the parent company insisted did publishers do so. They usually looked instead for songs with simpler melodies and commonplace lyrics. Well-written songs possessing any poetic qualities were rejected immediately, because it was the general Tin Pan Alley feeling that true sheet-music buyers had little or no interest in them and therefore they were "not commercial." Those "great" songs of the 1930s, beloved by cultural elitists and social historians, were well known only to a minority of Americans—those who were better educated and more affluent than the average radio "fan" and who had access to the Broadway stage and other sophisticated entertainment.

Technological changes, modern listening and buying habits, and the final displacement of vaudeville as the popular song's prime exploitation medium had forced some remodeling of the traditional hit-making procedures. However, many of Tin Pan Alley's original methods were still in use. As it had since the late nineteenth century, the process began when an "advance-artist" or "professional" copy of a pre-selected song was sent to the "hit-makers." In the late 1930s the most important of these were the people who selected music for coast-to-coast broadcast performances—not only performers but employees of the networks and of radio-advertising agencies and recording companies. Persons called upon to promote songs were known as "plugs," the word being both a noun and a verb. The major plugs were performers on commercial network broadcasts, their producers and musical directors, and those who played or sang on unsponsored broadcasts. Among the last were radio-station staff vocalists, who earned $25 a week and were heard after 5:00 p.m. (but before the commercial shows went on), and bandleaders whose "remote" programs were heard after 11:00 p.m., when all national advertising came to an end. Performances by these plugs were as important as those on commercial broadcasts because they enjoyed equal value on "the sheet."

In the later 1930s, Tin Pan Alley renewed its interest in recordings, reflecting the new importance of an industry that had witnessed many changes since the early days when a vocalist or musician usually selected the popular songs to be recorded. The "Artists and Repertoire" or "A&R" men employed by companies like RCA Victor or Columbia Records (the latter purchased in 1938 by the Columbia Broadcasting System for $750,000) had complete control of all recorded music and the manner in which it was performed by artists—whom they had also selected. The one with the most flair and genuine talent was Jack Kapp of Decca Records, who had been in the business since he was a teen-ager. Kapp's approach to record-making was expressed by a placard hanging from the neck of a cigar-store Indian on display in his main studio; it asked "Where's the melody?"—a question that pointed up the industry-wide reluctance to take any chances on music that might disturb record-buyers, a reluctance that resulted in the generally homogenized best-selling recordings each label offered.

Kapp had British backing to found Decca Records, which opened for business in 1934, using an English firm's name and having access to its master recordings. American Decca's output was intended primarily for the newly revived nickel juke-box business, but its discs were also offered to the public for 35 cents each, or three for a dollar, at a time when the standard price was 75 cents for a ten-inch popular recording. The coin-operated machine was in the newest stage of development from the simple device created in 1890 by an Edison dictating-machine franchise-holder, who discovered that people would pay to hear music through tubes not unlike a doctor's stethoscope attached to a cylinder-playing machine, and placed his devices around the San Francisco Bay area. Electrically powered, coin-operated record-playing machines first became available in 1930; nine years later 300,000 of them were in daily use, earning a nickel for each play and consuming three out of every five of the nearly 45 million discs manufactured that year.

Kapp's success demonstrated that better times were possible for the industry. His recording by Bing Crosby of *Sweet Leilani* sold over 100,000 copies; that of *A Tisket A Tasket* with

Ella Fitzgerald in 1938 sold 200,000. This new high was followed by RCA Victor's *Beer Barrel Polka* (made from a European master), which Kapp "covered" with an Andrews Sisters version; the two releases enjoyed a combined sale of 300,000 copies. Tin Pan Alley began to look on A & R men with new regard.

Once record men and other "hit-makers" indicated a favorable response to a song—and only a quarter of the songs submitted to them got one—a promotion campaign of 10 to 15 weeks followed. Regular edition piano-vocal copies and stock dance-band arrangements were made and immediately rushed off to recording executives and radio-station staff vocalists. Other copies were carried or mailed to the 200 "name bands" around the country that enjoyed regional or national prominence. After a few weeks, the songpluggers went into Phase Two, a period of about one month devoted to "working the song" by securing broadcast performances.

Most large New York music houses had staffs of three to seven songpluggers in the home offices and others in smaller broadcasting production centers. Only the 300 members of the Music Publishers Contact Employees Union were authorized by organized labor to deal with the AFL-affiliated musicians and radio performers. Staff songpluggers were paid $75 to $150 a week plus $25 to $75 for expenses, which were carefully controlled. Their bosses, the "professional managers" in charge of all exploitation and promotion, received $200 to $250 a week plus expenses. The contact employees

> wooed bandleaders with such varied gifts as liquor, theater and baseball tickets, clothes, women, jewelry, resort vacations, musical arrangements for their bands, and just plain money. . . . Some bandleaders were constantly taking; others were just as constantly refusing. . . . Some publishers treated the leaders with courtesy, respect and consideration; others merely plowed bullishly ahead, intent only on getting one particular plug for the tune. . . .

> The bandleaders weren't blameless either—not by a long shot. Some relished the warped attention they received. At times their demands for favors exceeded the ridiculous. And many publishers bitterly resented the "publishers' nights" and "official openings" at which they were expected to appear, generally with large entourages, all for the benefit of the band.[20]

A crucial decision had to be made before Phase Two came to an end: whether or not to keep on plugging. Unless faltering sheet-music sales indicated that the song was a "dog" doomed to failure despite all exploitation, all decks were cleared for the culmination of the campaign to boost the plug song to the "top of the sheet." This was done over a seven-day period appropriately known as "drive week." A final concentrated effort squeezed out every possible radio performance. The publisher and his professional manager handled the major radio shows; the job of persuading remote-broadcast bandleaders to feature the song while they were "on the air" from hotels, dance halls, nightclubs, ballrooms, and other venues was given to the troops, the lowly songpluggers, on whom "the pressure was intense. They had to produce or lose their jobs. . . ."[21]

Following "drive week," songplugging gradually tapered off over a period of about a month. A new candidate for "hitdom," for the title of "Number One Plug Song," was being chosen and the hit-making machine was preparing for new action.

After making a study of the hit-making procedures at this time, Duncan MacDougald, Jr. concluded that they were

> . . . largely borrowed from those being used by any industry producing consumer goods which do not strictly belong to the necessities of life. The promotion and distribution of popular songs is not left to chance nor to the spontaneous success or failure of the material offered in the market. What makes this process so similar to the industrial one is its highly developed "system," all of whose parts are directed toward one end: the enforcement of the material on the customer. As a result of various circumstances, this systematic character today has reached a stage where the exploitation of songs has become largely automatic.[22]

Lest the reader gain too doleful an impression of the state of American popular music in the late Thirties because of the procedures thus described, an important point must be made. Two thousand songs *were* published annually in regular copies by the large houses, but only 350-500 of them enjoyed exploitation by the machine and its mechanic songpluggers. Of these, about 100 made some stir. A 70,000-copy sale made a song a "hit"; only about 20 songs went over the 100,000 mark, five reaching the then-phenomenal figure of 300,000 (considering a shelf-life of six to at most nine months). More importantly, they were the songs best known to Americans because of their use on radio. There were also many thousands of other songs that appeared in printed form of some kind and/or on phonograph recordings, as did other types of music in which Tin Pan Alley had little or no interest, chiefly because they, too, were "not commercial," that is, would not sell as sheet music in quantities sufficient to warrant their exploitation.

The Great ASCAP-Radio War of 1941

On 1 August 1940, in a letter "to all advertisers" Gene Buck, the president of ASCAP, wrote: ". . . no question as to which came first, the 'hen or the egg'—*music made radio* instead of radio making music."

It was an issue that would soon be joined.

The relationship between radio and ASCAP, growing ever more symbiotic in the years from 1922 to 1939, had been marked by constant argumentation, mutual harassment, and conflict. Various broadcaster elements sought to change the copyright laws. They lobbied for local statutes limiting the Society's activities. They endeavored to build an image of ASCAP as a monopoly (which indeed it had become) and urged the federal government to take anti-trust action. They complained constantly about rising performance-rights fees, for from 1932 on ASCAP had begun to see radio as more than a nominal fee-payer—one in fact which could make up losses of income to the Society from falling sheet-music sales and record royalties. Agreements had been forged calling for payments of 2% of revenue from the sales of advertising time; the figure had risen to 5% in 1936, in a contract expiring at the end of 1940. In 1938, Neville Miller, the president of the National Association of Broadcasters (NAB), which had been formed way back in 1923 to deal with the Society, said that music was still his organization's major problem in spite of all efforts to achieve a peaceful solution. Now was the time for the industry to do something about ASCAP.

After a number of trial-balloon statements warning that broadcast-performance fees might double, in early 1940 the Society presented an industry that was united on few issues other than music licensing new contracts to take effect 1 January 1941. They offered license-fee reductions of one-third to one-half to independent stations, but asked the networks, NBC and CBS, which were already paying through the stations they owned and operated, to pay in addition 7½% of all receipts from sale of *network* advertising time, less certain deductions. The networks flatly refused. Moreover, years of unfortunate customer relations in dealing with broadcasters, later conceded by the Society to have been ill conceived, took their toll: a majority of both independent and network-affiliated stations joined the networks in refusing the new terms. At midnight on 31 December 1940, after negotiations had broken down completely, all ASCAP music went off the air over most stations in the United States. (A small number of broadcasters, well known for their iron-willed refusal to run with the pack, or else anticipating special concessions for their action when the conflict ended, effected a licensing arrangement with the Society.)

In anticipation of just such a "music war," the radio industry had organized in late 1939 an alternate source of music, Broadcast Music, Inc. (BMI), whose largest source of financial support was the networks. The organization had been financed by the sale, to FCC licensees only, of stock from which, as was stated in papers filed with the Securities and Exchange Commission, dividends were not anticipated. Like ASCAP, BMI intended to distribute, after deducting for its operating expenses, fees for performance to the copyright owners of music it licensed. However, unlike ASCAP, BMI offered to pay a basic rate of one penny each for all performances of copyrighted music, whether live or recorded, network or local. ASCAP did not yet recognize the playing of commercially recorded music as a "performance," and it based half of all its payments to publishers on network-broadcast performances, the balance on other non-performance criteria. Payments to songwriters were based in part on live network performances, in part on the writer's prestige, seniority, and size of catalogue licensed by the Society.[23]

The framers of the blueprint for BMI's structure and operation knew that the major ASCAP music houses issued approximately 2,000 new songs each year, of which only about 100 achieved measurable success. They also knew from study of the Society's 1938 performances that about 2,500 selections had supplied almost 85% of all the music required by the networks, which were being asked to pay most of the proposed ASCAP fees and would necessarily do the same to support BMI.

To be successful, BMI had to find songwriters who had not been admitted to ASCAP membership but were capable of writing the kind of popular music expected by professional music publishers. And it seemed there were such writers available because of the Society's discriminatory membership requirements, which asked for evidence of at least five successful songs before a writer could be considered for membership. The involvement of professional music publishers, whether affiliated with ASCAP or not, was equally necessary. The true secret, however, for the success of any attempt to go on the air without ASCAP repertoire would ultimately depend on the extent to which broadcasters could retrieve control of their own program-content by taking over the song-exploitation process already in place.

Activated in February 1940, BMI had eleven months before the December 31 deadline when all ASCAP music might be off the air. All its time and effort went into preparing for that possibility, by working to (1) create a non-ASCAP catalogue of at least 1,000 new songs; (2) find another 1,500 non-ASCAP selections; and (3) with those important 2,500 selections available, bring in other new and old works by contracting with individual non-ASCAP publishing enterprises. Clearly, the last goal meant finding not only firms already in business but new ones whose owners had sound judgment as to the popularity-potential of new music, good contacts in the songwriting field, plus knowledge of the hit-making procedures and the administrative skill to use them effectively. There were many members of the Music Publishers Contact Employees Union who were capable but lacked the capital to publish and promote their own music. There was also another music business—generally disregarded—that dealt in non-Tin Pan Alley or Hollywood music; its catalogues were basically made up of music "published" only on recordings, including both "race" and "hillbilly," as well as other types that had already attained popularity among various social, racial, economic, and cultural American minorities.

By providing financial support in the form of advances against future earnings, BMI assisted in the creation of new publishing companies. Musicians and bandleaders, for example, quickly learned that it was not a complex matter to copyright and publish their own compositions and then offer them for public performance through BMI. And, to the anger of their ASCAP associates, some publishers resigned from the Society and joined BMI, bringing their music along. Though most new BMI affiliates were drawn to it because of the financial support it offered to form new companies, there also were many whose catalogues of music already existed in basically recorded form, who entered into contractual agreements *only* because of BMI's promise to pay one cent for each *recorded* performance, which was becoming the major way in which their music could reach a larger public.

New York and California music-men scoffed at the notion of a broadcaster-built music catalogue to substitute for ASCAP's significant repertory. But they had forgotten their own recent trade history, or else failed to understand its implications. Five years earlier, in 1935, after a power struggle within the ASCAP circle of board-member publishers, the Warner Brothers motion-picture production group withdrew the entire body of music it owned and licensed through ASCAP and began to negotiate individual agreements with broadcasters. The eleven Warner Brothers music houses represented, according to which side counted, from 25 to 40% of the entire ASCAP catalogue. From January until late July 1936 the music of George Gershwin, Jerome Kern, Rudolph Friml, Sigmund Romberg, Victor Herbert, Cole Porter, Rodgers and Hart, Harry Warren, and many other successful writers was off the air on most stations; the networks—now the major component of the hit-making process—had refused to sign with Warner Brothers. Without those network plugs, Warner Brothers suffered a decline in box-office receipts from films using popular songs, and the sale of Warner Brothers music, which had amounted to $718,000 in the previous six months, fell to $299,000. In mid-1936 they returned to the ASCAP fold, where they continued their fight for a greater voice in Society operations—but now in the boardroom—and fought successfully enough to collect a major portion of the 1939 distribution of $2.5 million to music-publisher members.

This episode had apparently been forgotten by the publishing industry, and with it the evidence that radio audiences, conditioned by a regular flow of new songs getting extensive plugging, had not cared who wrote the music they heard and never realized the absence of the Warners' important catalogue, with its music of Gershwin, Porter, Rodgers and Hart, et al. The networks' appropriation of their own program-making decisions had also gone unnoticed by the public, which had little interest in the fact that others had taken over the hit-making procedures with which Tin Pan Alley had pioneered. These were major elements in the radio broadcasters' success in weathering the withdrawal of the entire ASCAP catalogue of music available in December 1940.[24]

Even an action by the United States government itself failed to end the standoff between the Society and the broadcasters. In late 1940 the Justice Department charged, in a civil suit, that all parties in the dispute—ASCAP, BMI, NBC, and CBS—were involved in anti-trust violations such as illegal pooling, price-fixing, various restraints of trade, mutual boycotts, and discrimination against composers and songwriters. (The litany of malfeasance smacked of the original Board of Music Trade trust and its practices.) In addition, a separate federal criminal suit—but against ASCAP alone—was brought, with the same charges. Within a month BMI signed a consent decree to settle the suit against itself and the broadcasting interests. A few weeks later ASCAP capitulated with a similar settlement resolving both the civil and criminal suits.

In 1941, losing nearly $300,000 each month, with its publisher members denied any access to network time and with income from new musical films declining, ASCAP surrendered in the great ASCAP-radio war. Contracts reducing the previously demanded rates were offered and accepted. The networks reached agreements calling for "blanket" licenses to pay fees of 2-3/4% of all sales of advertising time; local and independent stations agreed to pay 2-1/4, and the smaller daytime operations accepted contracts calling for even lower fees. With the war over, the music publishers, both the old-line houses and some of the newly formed ones, took the marvelous hit-making machine back from the broadcasters (who were only too happy to relinquish it for fear of possible anti-trust accusations). BMI had never seen itself as completely superseding ASCAP and was now content to commit itself to future service as a small version of the senior organization. It hoped to secure its own share of those important 2,500 selections that provided 85% of the networks' music programming. However time, a world war, new technology, changes in the American character, culture, social, and economic order; a baby boom and the consequent democratization, or populist re-orientation, of America's popular music—these were all to divert that modest ambition. For the moment—but only a brief one—America's marvelous hit-making music machine was returned to those who had created it and brought it to perfection: the historical publisher-ASCAP structure.

PAYING TO PLAY AND PLAYING FOR PAY: 1942-1980

The Music War Is Over: 1942

At the beginning of 1942, 19 of the 20 best-selling songs were ASCAP-licensed, and almost all of them had been written for films. During the ASCAP-radio war, Hollywood had failed to profit from any new musical motion picture, since its music could not be promoted on radio. Most of the costly new film musicals, in fact, had been held "in the can" until their songs could enjoy the blessings of on-the-air exploitation. The peace treaty had come just in time, for the stakes were great: if during the Depression a hit song had added more than $1 million to a film's gross receipts, the value of such hits had risen steadily since then.

The whole songplugging mechanism, which had been investigated by the Office of Radio Research and Duncan MacDougald prior to the ASCAP-radio break, was continuing to function as it had before the contretemps. Its purpose remained to lead the public at large, and specifically the radio audience,

> more and more to the point of merely accepting these songs as standardized [musical] products, with less and less active resentment and critical interest. While the accepted songs are being incessantly hammered into the listeners' heads, the prestige build-up strives to make the audience believe that this constant repetition is due to the inherent qualities of the song, rather than the will to sell it—either for prestige or profits. Thus it may be assumed that this controlled repetition and manipulated recommendation seem to tend to the standardization of the tastes of the listener and the subsequent gradual eradication of those tastes.[25]

Because of the new contracts which reduced broadcast license fees, ASCAP income fell by $1 million in 1942 and dropped again in 1943, but royalties from the $40 million sale of records in both years helped bridge part of the loss by songwriters and publishers of performing-rights income. Another significant change in the distribution of income accruing from sheet music and mechanical royalties had been effected by the SPA (Songwriters Protective Association) in 1939. Its new "Standard Uniform Popular Songwriters Contract," which was accepted by many more, though still not all, publishers, increased to 50% the minimum writer royalties from mechanical reproduction. And, in anticipation of the use of music on television, the publishers were precluded from licensing music for that medium without the writers' consent. Within a decade, due entirely to SPA, American songwriters had become almost first-class citizens of the music world, rather than the serfs that most of them had been throughout the nineteenth century and into the twentieth.

In a "think piece" analyzing the past year of 1941, *Variety* (7 January 1942, p. 155) consoled an industry still wrangling over the "radio war," pointing out that it had been a combination of the government's anti-trust actions against ASCAP and the Society's own "bad judgment" that had led to the major drop in performing-rights income. *Variety* added that BMI had been saved by its contracts with new and business-wise music publishers as well as two defectors from ASCAP, Edward B. Marks Music Corp. and Peer International Corporation, which supplied most of the Latin American popular songs that enjoyed success in 1940 and 1941. The government's criminal suit against ASCAP, initiated after "foot-dragging" in the anti-trust matter, settled by a plea of *nolo contendere*, proved to be the last straw for ASCAP publisher board-members, who now labelled songwriter-president Gene Buck's handling of the whole business as "inept." *Variety* reported further (29 April 1942, p. 41) that the board's tacit admission of criminal guilt could have been avoided had Buck reported exactly what the Justice Department wanted from the Society. With 11 publishers and 5 writers voting to do so, Buck was ousted with a pension.

The consent decree signed by ASCAP in March 1941 posed new problems for both the Society and the hit-making machine. The understanding called for abolition of ASCAP's self-perpetuating board of directors; an end to its requirement of five published works in order to be elected to membership; and a modification of the performance-payment criteria used in its distribution of income. With the membership standards loosened, 250 new writer and publisher members joined ASCAP by the summer of 1942. This larger base among which ASCAP income was dispensed led to an immediate drop in royalties paid to the 50 top-rated authors and composers, in fact a reduction by 25% from the $16,000 each had received for 1939. The major publishers, controlling the distribution of their own ASCAP money, however, did not sustain a similar loss. As the years passed, the rift widened between the dominant music publishers and the increasing number of new composers and authors, who grew out of all proportion to the major music houses. The future would include many additional court cases, private law suits, congressional investigations, government interventions, and other matters, all providing pastures of plenty for the legal profession. It would be two decades more before the Society entered an era of relative internal peace.

BMI and the Hit-Making Machine

Despite the part it had played in contributing to a reduction in ASCAP license fees, BMI faced an uncertain future in the summer of 1942. Broadcasters were undecided over continuing support for the organization, now that its basic mission had been accomplished. Many, however, felt that it should be continued at least until the war caused advertisers to slash their radio-ad budgets, which in turn would force the networks to effect economies. CBS and NBC had already saved over $10 million in proposed ASCAP license fees, and they could easily absorb the loss of $1.2 million in liabilities to copyright owners with which BMI had binding contracts should the new organization be closed down. Living on this knife-edge of indecision about its future, BMI continued to serve as a licensing agency, although it also published songs. To demonstrate its good financial situation, it doubled the penny-per-performance promised to its own writers in original contracts, while raising its publisher payments to 4 cents, a 400% increase. Dealing for public-performance rights chiefly with publishers, BMI expected that they would share that income with *their* writers on the basis of contractual understanding. This misperception of music publishers' liberality, together with ASCAP's revised distribution system (which tended to give more credit to performances than in the past), resulted in a greater flow of new writers to ASCAP than to BMI until well into the early 1950s.

Having lost its exclusive access to the song-exploitation system and now being content to assume the role of a mini-ASCAP, BMI determined to follow the traditional Tin Pan Alley route to success. It offered attractive guarantees and advances against future earnings to experienced music-men employed by ASCAP firms, expecting through them to provide a reasonably adequate share of the popular music on which network programming was based. (Its efforts to do so as a publisher, however, failed more often than they succeeded.)

Despite its financial support of New York- and Hollywood-based publishing ventures which could secure the network plugs that made hit songs, BMI finished a poor second to ASCAP during most of the 1940s. Its desperate quest for national performances was halted temporarily from time to time following revelations of "promotional excesses" by its affiliated publishers. The application of "pay for play" reached ridiculous proportions in 1945, when one BMI publisher took advantage of $48 offered for each network performance: he secured plugs of 60 very unfamiliar songs each evening, five times a week, on a half-hour network broadcast.[26]

Negotiations between the Music Publishers Protective Association and two rack-owning distributing companies insured repayment of the cost of launching a song as soon as it hit the "Top Twenty" sales charts in 1946. Dependence on conservative retail jobbers, who ordered only after they were certain a song was a blockbuster, was also decreased. Guaranteed orders of over 300,000 sheet-music copies for some 35,000 metal stands—placed in drug stores, newspaper and magazine stores, markets, and other locations—brought in over $50,000 before returns, if any, and added income from re-orders to the old-line houses which had all the hits.

A new and economically significant music world outside the old established system appeared by mid-1946. BMI's offer to pay for performances of music on commercial recordings had immediately attracted many disc artists and small publishers involved in hillbilly music, as the country-music idiom was then known. They, and others, working in culturally significant but economically minor musical genres, among them the race records intended for black audiences, were responding in increasing numbers to BMI's open invitation. After completing agreements, many received cash advances of several hundred dollars for each new recording produced. Consequently, BMI found itself providing more music to low-paying local stations than to the networks and their affiliates, as it became "the only game in town" for many catalogues distributed in quantity through recordings that its best customers refused to program. Unwittingly, the licensing body was creating the major repository of the black and country music from which rock-and-roll would spring.

The Music Business in the Courtroom During the 1940s

Despite the gains insuring a greater share in printed music and mechanical royalties made for them by the Songwriters Protective Association, most established Tin Pan Alley songwriters continued to have difficulties with their publishers. Contrary to the present copyright law, which grants protection for a piece of music the moment it is put down on paper or recorded, the 1909 act provided for full copyright and its privileges only after publication. This generally occurred once a contract had been signed by both writer and publisher, assigning all rights to the latter's control. The question as to who *controlled* the performing right of ASCAP composer and author members had never, however, been tested in court. As this issue became vitally important with the formation of BMI, *Variety* speculated that it had been avoided by the Society because a resolution might split writers and publishers into camps even more opposed than those already existent.[27]

Among the earliest publishers to affiliate with BMI in 1940 had been the veteran Edward B. Marks, who was dissatisfied with his company's rating in ASCAP and did not renew his membership in the Society. However, 5,000 to 6,000 Marks' songs, approximately 20% of his catalogue, were by ASCAP members, and presumably jointly owned with them. Waiting for court clarification of their status, BMI had not offered these songs for broadcast use. ASCAP continued to avoid resolution of performing rights' ownership, and in 1941, with BMI's support, Marks filed an action against the Society, contending that once a writer signed an initial publishing contract he had no further control over administration of the performing right. ASCAP responded that 50% of that right was retained by the songwriter.

In the opinion of many eminent entertainment-business attorneys, the publisher did indeed own all rights and the courts would so decide. It was anticipated that in such an event the composers and authors of popular music would realize that they shared in performance income only on the sufferance of the publishers, and they would consequently withdraw from the Society and form another, returning to the original concept underlying ASCAP's formation, that of a body of creators of music banding together to control their performing rights themselves. Should the decision go the other way, it was assumed that the creators of music would take control of ASCAP, throw out the publishers, and distribute to themselves alone all collections from radio networks and stations, motion-picture theaters, and other music-users. In either event, the Society was expected to undergo traumatic changes when the action was concluded.

The defendant licensing society had refused to settle the suit by giving publisher and writer members non-exclusive rights, contending that songwriters still controlled their music even if their publisher resigned from ASCAP to join BMI. Publishers regarded this rather uneasily: if ASCAP won, they would occupy a secondary position at best within the Society.

After four years' legal delay, during which offstage efforts were made to remove the matter from judicial determination, the case of *Marks vs. ASCAP* came to trial. In late April 1945, the court found that, once rights had been assigned, transfer of them could be made only with the consent of all parties involved—composer, author, and publisher. Also, any agreement involving royalties must be made for the benefit of all parties concerned, or else it constituted a breach of contract. Though the motion-picture industry-connected firms wished for a reversal of the findings, they did not pursue an appeal, and the Solomon-like decision aborted a predicted dramatic change in ASCAP structure.

Licensing of music for television had also become by this time a matter of ASCAP concern. Many writers had already granted these rights to the Society, but the motion-picture company-owned publishers would not do so, having been made aware that presentation of feature films on television would seriously affect their parent companies. Dissension over this matter, which was making it impossible for ASCAP to offer licenses to the networks for use of its catalogue, was to insure BMI's continuing existence. The Society had been charging each television broadcaster a token $1 a year for all music rights while experimental telecasting was taking place, but now that regular programming was available, the motion-picture industry-owned publishers still refused to assign those rights, and, since negotiations with NBC and CBS were prolonged as a result, any new arrangement seemed impossible. Suddenly regarded in a new light by major customers who had been ready to cast it adrift, BMI was expected to fill the void should another music war develop over the use of ASCAP music on television. Consequently, in September 1947, the networks extended their BMI contracts through the year 1959.

Another court action involving ASCAP was to assist BMI in extending its licenses to independent radio broadcasters beyond the 1949 expiration date. After having hiked movie-theater license fees by 300%, ASCAP lost a major court case brought against it by a group of film exhibitors who charged that because the Society controlled all music used in film synchronization, they were required to pay for the entire ASCAP catalogue rather than for just the small number of selections they used. The Society was found to be a monopoly operating in restraint of trade, but the decision did not specify whether its monopolistic practices referred only to the licensing of movie theaters or its entire operation.[28] ASCAP did not appeal the decision and there was no further clarification of the ruling. However, ASCAP could no longer license motion-picture exhibitors, and the loss of an estimated $3.5 million from these theaters faced the Society, leading many independent broadcasters to fear that they would be expected to make up the deficit in new, and higher ASCAP license fees. This was the major factor in their acceptance of an extended BMI license a few months after the networks had approved a similar agreement.

BMI could now look forward to a fiscally sound future. Neither an increase in broadcaster rates nor another music war took place, and for that matter both ASCAP and BMI income continued to rise annually.

BMI and the New Independent Local Stations

An immediate problem facing Carl Haverlin, BMI's first paid full-time chief executive, who took office on 15 April 1947 (his predecessors having been involved only on a part-time basis and often without compensation other than fees and/or expenses), had been the forthcoming expiration, within a few years, of the original broadcaster contract.[29] Some network executives had questioned renewal because of BMI's failure consistently to deliver hits; other radio industry leaders believed that BMI should be reorganized as a separate corporation, free from all ties to radio. ASCAP's own legal problems and wrangling by members resolved the problem within less than a year after Haverlin had assumed his office.

Announcing that it would stand on its own feet, under Haverlin's direction BMI sought to divorce itself of a general perception as being "the creature of the networks," which owned 20% of BMI non-dividend stock and used 10 to 15% of its music on television, perhaps twice that on radio. Although BMI continued its efforts (which were generally unproductive) to increase network usage of its repertoire, it paid greater attention to the country's independent stations and the music they were using. Following the lifting in 1945 of the Federal Communications Commission's wartime freeze on station licensing and construction, these stations had begun to grow in number until by 1950 there were 1,517 (half in single-station markets), as compared to 627 network affiliates, and they relied chiefly on a music-and-news program format. Unable to compete with the experienced and established network affiliates, but recognizing the growing appeal to their local audiences of country music and rhythm-and-blues, many of these independent stations increased their use of both. Viewing television as an enemy that would eventually drive all radio programming into bankruptcy, most of them operated on a shoestring, with inexperienced young disc-jockey talent. The country-music and rhythm-and-blues popularity charts on which their music selection was based were dominated by BMI, provided to the organization by firms that had been established during 1941 and new ones (which BMI was now actively recruiting) that were being formed by recently organized record companies.

Haverlin and BMI management made the first meaningful effort to create a system of pay-ments to writers besides those whose music the licensing body itself published. Occasionally, in response to queries from the music trade press, BMI officials had declared their intention to establish some means of direct payment to songwriters and composers, in addition to the usual payments to publishers alone. But even as late as November 1948 it was common knowledge in the business that most BMI firms did not pay writers of the music that BMI licensed, despite BMI's expectation that they would do so. In 1949, the first payment system to "affiliated" writers was instituted, and it was revised and improved on later occa-sions. BMI admitted to affiliation status, and continues to do so, any author and composer whose work, "susceptible of performance," is published by a BMI-affiliated publisher.

Radio, the Dee Jay, and the Record Business in the 1940s

Throughout the 1930s the American Federation of Musicians (AFM) was adamant in its opposition to radio's use of recorded music on the air, correctly anticipating that "canned" music would lead to the displacement of live musicians. The union's drive to control "electrically transcribed/for one-time use only" sponsored programs culminated successfully in 1937; in return for permission to use these cheaper "E.T." substitutes for live programming, the networks agreed to employ fixed quotas of union musicians, their number related to the broadcaster's income, and to eschew all use of commercially recorded discs. A number of large stations, however, rented union-approved transcribed libraries of individual selections. And half of the country's 700 stations in the 1930s, with income too small to concern the union, continued to play records for their local audiences.

In 1938 the AFM first entered into licensing agreements with the major record companies, requiring them to include the phrases "for home use only" or "not licensed for radio broadcast" on all discs, hoping thus to stop small broadcasters from using them. In 1940 an appeals court ruled, in the case of one bandleader who had sued radio stations for violating the injunctions on the use of his music, that artists did indeed have common-law copyrights in their recordings of songs, but that this right ended with the sale of the records: having purchased them, broadcasters had no further obligation to either artist or manufacturer. This ruling was completely unexpected by the record companies, some of which were already preparing to license the use of their discs to broadcasters in return for substantial fees. But the Supreme Court refused to review the lower court's decision and it stood. The door was open for the age of the "dee jay"—the record-spinning disc jockey, host on radio programs built on a repertory of recorded music.

Martin Block and his *Make-Believe Ballroom*, first broadcast over WNEW-AM, New York, on 3 February 1935, had already demonstrated the commercial viability of recorded-music programming by large metropolitan radio stations. WNEW had no phonograph records in its library, so Block bought some dance-music platters and played them from an imaginary dance hall while engaging in equally imaginary conversation with the bandleader. [30] Because WNEW's sales department was not convinced of the program's format as a vehicle for effective advertising, Block was forced to peddle his show to sponsors. Within four months, four million New York-area listeners were tuning in on his twice-daily highly personalized segments of music by bandleaders and vocalists. After WNEW successfully introduced an all-night record program, *The Milkman's Matinee*, the future was clear to imaginative program directors on non-network stations.

Throughout the 1920s, record companies had actively sought boosting of their product by radio. With the industry's general adoption in 1925 of electrical recording to supplant Thomas Edison's now half-century-old acoustic technology, the quest for radio use became easier, as the quality of recordings was improved and they became suitable for broadcast use. Victor Records, in particular, used radio to promote its new releases. Early in 1925 the single broadcast of an unreleased John McCormack recording of Irving Berlin's *All Alone* resulted in an immediate rush of orders for 150,000 copies. Two years later Victor's president said that broadcasters' use of selected releases resulted in an "immediate and traceable demand" for them.[31] However, after industry sales tumbled because of the sagging economy from the $75 million of 1929 to less than $17 million two years later, many executives began to express their belief that radio use was responsible for the significant decline. The few active recording companies abandoned any radio-station servicing policy. Victor, still the industry giant, dropped all promotion of its popular product and concentrated on the "Red Seal" concert music that had brought it the acclaim of educators and opinion-makers (but never more than 20% of total record sales since 1903, when the label was first used). Like most others, Victor employed an elementary distribution system, selling to a distributor (whose business it owned), who in turn sold to retailers at about 40% discount. Nothing was done at the national level to promote individual releases of popular dance music other than mailings of review copies to the trade press and the music editors of selected newspapers and general-interest magazines. All broadcaster and disc-jockey promotion was left to the local distributor and retailer, and to the music publishers, recording artists, and their publicity and promotion people. As late as 1955, RCA Victor still charged its own distributors for the promotional kits and records they began to send to radio stations after World War II.

The first significant change in the record manufacturers' exploitation procedures was made by Capitol Records, formed in 1943 on an original investment of $10,000. From the start, Capitol sent personalized special copies of new releases to key disc jockeys. In 1969, Glenn Wallichs, one of Capitol's founders, reminisced: "We typed special labels with their names on both sides, pressed them on expensive, lightweight, unbreakable, vinylite compound, and then had our limited employee force drive around and distribute each sample personally. It was an event that created a sensation."[32] Promoting its product aggressively on radio by means of disc-jockey play, within five years Capitol was regarded as a major manufacturer, the equal of Columbia, RCA Victor, and Decca, which now were imitating its exploitation techniques. The provision of records to disc jockeys without charge was in a historical sense an innovative change similar to that of the first Tin Pan Alley men to give their music, in copies printed for the purpose, to vaudeville performers and bandleaders, hoping to obtain exploitation of their product. Both practices led to further cost-free services, and finally, of course, to paying-for-play.

Collections of pre-war 78-r.p.m. dance and vocal music no longer sufficed for the large group of new broadcasters and other non-network stations who had to supply all their own programming; their audiences seemed to prefer new kinds of music performed by new artists, available principally from the hundreds of new, small, independent recording companies. First in order of appeal to local listeners was the old-time hillbilly music (but now with an up-to-date sound) which many Americans had discovered during the war, with its population shifts which had introduced many of them to new regional and ethnic minority cultures. Next was the music written and performed by black artists, and intended for black audiences, which was now attracting young whites of both sexes. This too had a modern sound, coming from the infusion into the older "race" music of elements of jazz, swing, boogie-woogie, and gospel, blended with a liberal mix of urban black-ghetto pop-blues.

A shortage of materials and the first strike by the American Federation of Musicians against the recording industry, from 1942 to late 1944, had caused Columbia and RCA Victor to cut down on their black-music production. Postwar competition from the new independents now forced them to resume it. But because the music was no longer the old "race" product they had pioneered, they had little success competing with the more knowledgeable newcomers, though they did succeed in driving many of the smaller operations out of business. The story was different in the country-music field, production of which they had halted only temporarily. With postwar peace they resumed manufacture for the southern retail and jukebox trade, and as the songs began to "cross over" into the popular field, they increased production and began to sign newcomers to the field.

Among the founders of the independent record companies created to fill the vacuum left by the major labels' withdrawal from the black-music business were jazz record collectors, record retailers catering to blacks, and suppliers to black-ghetto jukeboxes. Most of them intended only to provide records for fellow jazz fanatics or local and regional commercial markets. To keep costs down and avoid paying royalties for mechanical reproduction of copyrighted music, some of them did "what everybody else had always done" in dealing with artists (who often wrote their own material): they simply took over all rights to the music recorded.

The practice was an old one. In the 1920s, when the recording industry first found sizable markets among various racial and ethnic minorities, it had adopted a general policy of not recording any copyrighted music; rather, it signed artists who could write their own music or who used popular or folk music that could be put over as new songs. Most of this material was sold for a few dollars or assigned to the manufacturer as part of the recording agreement. The music went into "file-cabinet" publishing companies owned by the manufacturer or one of its employees.

Borrowing this procedure, the post-World War II independents created their own "desk-drawer" publishing houses, with the proprietor or a record supervisor often named as the songwriter, or co-writer. Black creative artists, untutored in copyright law with its bundle of rights, acquiesced without complaint. Many felt—as had race, hillbilly, and jazz talent throughout the 1920s and 1930s—that what counted was the publicity following a record release, which boosted fees for personal appearances (their largest source of income). There were, of course, some enlightened manufacturers who worked out more equitable financial arrangements with the artists and songwriters whose music they used; virtually none of them, however, offered SPA's "Uniform Popular Songwriters' Contract." This, incidentally, had been improved again in 1947 by obligating a publisher to exploit any music acquired from an SPA member. Many types of printed materials which had previously been royalty-free now received a minimum 10% royalty. The publisher was also required to publish piano versions and dance orchestrations, as well as to secure a commercial recording. If he failed to comply with these provisions within a year, the song reverted to its writer.

Recording technology went through a number of major changes in the late 1940s. First was the reel-to-reel tape recorder, which had been liberated from its German developers and brought home as Yank war booty, and was to prove a major element in the success of independent recording companies. The tape machine was portable; its magnetic ribbons were easy to edit, and corrections of flawed performances or misspoken lyrics, impossible on the earlier glass-based master recordings, were easy to make and effectively reduced production costs. As tape equipment became more affordable, new recording studios sprang up around the nation. Many of the independents acquired tape machines themselves and learned recording techniques not only in studios but nightclubs, theaters, dance halls, auditoriums, and even garages or men's rooms (where often a fine reverb effect offered a new sound for the new music). As a result of these developments, the free-wheeling independents were now providing competition that could not be disregarded by Columbia, Decca, RCA Victor, and the new Capitol label, which prior to 1948 accounted for three-fourths of all record sales.

The introduction of additional new technology rekindled old communications-business antagonisms. Responding to CBS's introduction of the 33-1/3-r.p.m. long-playing microgroove records in the spring of 1948, RCA Victor brought out a 45-r.p.m. disc to counter its ancient rival. A "battle of the speeds" was joined, to be resolved two years later when the CBS "LP" became standard for collections of songs and extended popular, theater, concert, and jazz works, while RCA's "45" became the standard for "singles"—individual pop songs. The traditional 78-r.p.m. disc went the way of the early cylinder, after RCA had spent $5 million to persuade the industry to adopt its new slow-playing platter.

Radio, Records, and the Old and New Tin Pan Alleys

As advertisers began to turn to the growing and increasingly devoted television audience, the resultant reduction of radio-network dramatic, variety, and musical fare posed major programming problems for the networks' affiliated stations. Generally sharing live talent with their sister television operations, they were important outlets for promoting the music from the major national production centers, New York and Hollywood, which had formerly been feeding them. Just as the networks' flagship stations, owned and operated by them, were doing in the face of rising operating costs and the competition for audiences from the independent record-playing stations, so too did the affiliated stations (which had once relied solely on the networks for nighttime programming) turn to the part-time use of recorded music. It was not uncommon to hear such disparate personalities as Jackie Robinson, Paul Whiteman, Leopold Stokowski, Arthur Treacher, Benny Goodman, Sam Goldwyn, H. V. Kaltenborn, and Tommy Dorsey presiding as platter-spinners over programs of recorded music broadcast by high-powered stations.

Faced with the inevitability of this national turn to recorded music, BMI had abandoned premium payments for live network-radio performances in favor of key disc-jockey play. ASCAP first included record performances in its distributions some years after 1949, when NBC had become the last major network to adopt the use of commercial discs on the air.

In 1950-51 nine major New York music publishers, including some that had been in the business for more than half a century, spent almost three times their record-royalty income for "exploitation." They received $636,897.53 in royalties from the sale of 33,713,751 recordings; they spent $1,682,773.53 for promotion.[33] Sheet-music sales had fallen despite the rack-retailing agreement; only the top handful of hit songs moved at all, and these were fortunate if they sold 200,000 copies. As a result, the major houses began to discount the importance of sheet-music sales and to regard some fifty disc jockeys in key major markets as being possessed with the power to make a hit. The hot medium was no longer print, as it had been when radio performers and bandleaders made the hits, but plastic, supplied by seven or eight record manufacturers.

Many owners of the stations where these dee jays thrived, lost in the strange world of popular music, left all selection of musical program-content to their top platter-spinners. Not only were they expert in the field; they also seemed to be the intimates of nationally famous recording stars, who deluged them and their secretaries with phone calls and tokens of friendship in the pursuit of new-product promotion.

Smaller broadcasting operations were of no interest to the New York and Hollywood publishers, which relied on large station plugs. Their dee jays, who "related" to listeners only a little younger than themselves, chose music from records delivered by the United States Postal Service or non-unionized songpluggers, the record companies' promotion men. Influenced by the trade-paper charts, manufacturers' reports of local sales, and/or small gifts of cash or other forms of gratuity handed out by the "promo men," the tyro platter-spinners soon were expert in the new music and the folkways of the independents.

In spite of this flourishing musical activity on independent American radio stations, the picture was dark for the established New York and Hollywood music-publishing business. The sale of sheet music had declined dramatically, and record sales had leveled off below the 1947 all-time high of $214.4 million; moreover, many more music publishers and songwriters were sharing in the distribution of a maximum of 2 cents per disc-side in mechanical royalties. Only shares in the increasing revenue earned by ASCAP made it possible for most of the Society's publishing-company members to survive, and then principally because of the network television performances they were able to obtain by plugging. ASCAP income had risen from about $5 million in 1940 to around $20 million in 1954, but over 80% of it came from radio and television broadcasters. After operating expenses were subtracted, some 55% of ASCAP publishers' share of remaining income was distributed on the basis of current performances on network television, network radio having become a minor factor. Writers, on the other hand, received 20% of their ASCAP income from performances on network television and such radio-network programming as still existed, as well as from spot-checks of major local independent radio stations which hewed to a straight middle-of-the-road music programming policy. The remainder of ASCAP income was distributed on the basis of non-performance factors, such as seniority, availability, and some built-in cushions to prevent drastic falls in income. The element of "seniority" more than doubled payments to songs that were more than two years old—such great ASCAP "standards" as *Stardust*, *Tea for Two*, *Sunny Side of the Street*, *Easter Parade*, *White Christmas*, and the like. Many other factors were also involved in higher ASCAP payouts: whether a song was a fall-winter hit, played when the major network programs were on the air; or whether it was a ballad (ballads being preferred over instrumental numbers, rhythm tunes, and novelties by network programmers, because they remained popular for longer periods and thus were better known to large masses of audiences).

Because their economic existence was at stake, the major music publishers turned their complete attention to securing performances on network television, effectively losing interest in independent radio stations and their disc jockeys, and in the music that half of all the people in the country—those under 25—were finding attractive. That decision proved to be highly profitable for a time, at least to the half dozen firms to which, as *Variety* pointed out, the big performance money was going:

> . . . The Warner Bros. combine, the Music Publishers Holding Corp., gets about $1,400,000 annually from ASCAP, while the Big Three (Robbins, Feist & Miller) and the Chappell combine receive around $800,000 a piece, with Mills Music and Shapiro-Bernstein Music not far behind. It's estimated that about six top ASCAP publishers get 75% of the publishers' take. Last year [1953], the ASCAP melon for publishers was $7,500,000. [34]

Turning their backs on radio-broadcasting activities between the Hudson River and the Los Angeles foothills, the six music publishers found a welcome from television performers and producers. Most of the medium's musical stars were old friends, radio artists now working in front of a camera and continuing to sing the standard ASCAP music they had featured in the past. Anxious to increase audiences and maintain high ratings, television producers looked for music that would satisfy the above-25 viewers who bought sets and kept a firm hand on the tuning dial in prime-time hours, when variety, musical, and light music programs occupied nearly 40% of the time on the national networks. In a single sample period, the third week of January 1955, 85 hours from 7:00 p.m to 11:00 p.m. were devoted to music and to variety programs of which music was a major ingredient. [35]

Documents submitted during hearings for a change in the copyright law proposed that year showed that the popular music establishment, essentially the members of the MPPA, were spending nearly $3 million annually just in salaries of employees whose sole duty was to plug and exploit their material. [36] (There were, of course, many other costs for that function.)

As television's income from sponsors grew, so too did the stakes in the video-payola game. Conceding that television did not present the same opportunities as had radio in the old days when bandleaders called their own tunes, *Variety* noted:

> The last pay-off to writers and publishers on video tune performances is turning into a new spawning-ground for payola and the cut-in. Under ASCAP's distribution formula, a plug on TV is worth three times the value of a radio plug, so that if a tune is performed on a 75-station TV hookup, it would rack up around 225 logging points or around $75 a day for both publishers and writers.
>
> Cases have already cropped up where music directors on video shows have put the arm on writers and/or publishers for plugging their tunes. If video plugs on a tune can be delivered on a regular basis, the payoff to the musical director can amount to one-half the writer's or the publisher's share.
>
> The video performance bonanza makes it a profitable thing all around to cut in anybody who can deliver the plugs. Some ASCAPites, despite the payoffs to third parties, have been hitting the big money in the dividend checks on cross-the-board TV shows. The same ethical considerations in all other payola practices also apply to the TV field: if it's profitable, it's okay.[37]

The more populist-inclined Tin Pan Alley that had taken shape—away from the New York and Hollywood film-music industry, away from television which was not interested in its music except for novelty appeal or its ability to deliver large audiences of young people during rating periods—now extended throughout the United States and included more than 600 of a new kind of "publisher." The major manufacturers pressed his records, but he used his own distribution and promotion system; and the local-station disk jockey was the chief booster of his product. During this decentralization of the popular-music industry and an ensuing populist reorientation of American music, the old established publishers completely relinquished their hold on the radio hit-making process. Their traditional consort, network radio broadcasting, had retired completely from the game, and television would be incapable of taking radio's place. By its very nature and the economics involved, the new video medium resisted that "publicizing by constant repetition" of new songs that is at the heart of the plugging procedure.[38]

In the early 1950s, hits recorded by independent manufacturers which appeared on *Billboard*'s rhythm-and-blues sales charts began occasionally to turn up also on the pop charts, those representing sales to the white market only. Once they began to do so, the major manufacturers moved quickly to "cover" them, using well-scrubbed white performers who originally borrowed the black performances, arrangements, and vocal phrasings—sometimes with such accuracy that legal action was threatened by the original performers or recording companies. Gradually these white-carbon duplicates took on a more sanitized, smoothed-out, slick, and easier-to-take quality as the large labels, with their national distribution chains, were able to crowd the original versions off the best-selling charts. Among the cover records were several made by Bill Haley, a white bandleader who played a combination of country-and-western, dixieland, and old-time rhythm-and-blues. In 1955 Haley recorded *Rock Around the Clock*, borrowed in large part from a number of old "race" blues but written by white songwriters. Despite its all-Caucasian creative involvement, this Number One pop vocal hit of 1955 crossed over to the top of the rhythm-and-blues charts and had some success in the country-music field as well.

Responding to the success of *Rock Around the Clock* and others in the same idiom, the major manufacturers went full-tilt into the teen-age and young adult market with their own kind of laundered rock-and-roll music—generally bland, up-tempo material that sought to emulate the real thing but was also expected to appeal to older buyers. This activity was reported on *Billboard*'s "Top 10" singles chart, introduced 2 November 1955 and renamed the "Hot 100" in August 1958. Here Frank Sinatra, Eddie Fisher, Teresa Brewer, Mitch Miller, Sammy Davis, Jr., and the like shared listings with exponents of the source music--Chuck Berry, Little Richard, Fats Domino, Joe Turner, Ray Charles, and their peers. In 1955, total record sales rose for the first time above the 1947 high of $214,400,000 (to $277 million); and within four years, with considerable help from a white Mississippi-born singer, the figure would double.

Living in the shadow of a more glamorous corporate stablemate, television, the ruling hierarchy of the successful but highly conservative RCA Victor record company was most interested in signing vocal talent with a potential for the electronic camera's scrutiny. Their stated public policy was to produce eight sides of "what the public wants" for every two of the Red Seal classical releases that had first given the firm a reputation for "quality" after 1904, but there was a lot of playing-safe in their artists-and-repertoire selection. For example, in spite of the parent corporation's splendid financial position, much of it due to the manufacture of television sets and equipment, Victor executives were reluctant to spend the $35,000 asked for an unclassifiable singer with the improbable name of Elvis Presley. (Columbia had already refused to go above $25,000 for his services.) RCA's resident "show-business figure" advisers predicted that the youth who sang country music with a country sound, black music with a black one, and popular music with a blend of both would never be successful on television. The Aberbach brothers, Jean and Julian, the majority owners of BMI's Hill & Range Songs, Inc., and also of several ASCAP firms, put together the package that brought Presley to RCA Victor. According to Arnold Shaw, the recording company "ostensibly put up $25,000 for Presley's recording contract while the Aberbachs paid $15,000 for publishing rights and the purchase of Hi Lo Music," the company that

owned songs Presley had already recorded for Sun Records of Memphis.[39] Hill & Range
Songs, Inc., also wound up administering Presley's BMI-affiliated Elvis Presley Music Corp.
as well as his ASCAP member company, Gladys Music, Inc., both of which published many
of the songs the superstar recorded. RCA got an artist who sold 28 million units in the
next two years, accounting for 31 of its 39 million-selling singles in that period, and who was
responsible for a quarter of the company's business in the next decade, according to
industry estimates.

TV producer and host, Ed Sullivan, in his quest for material to satisfy a mammoth television
audience and to maintain top ratings for his Sunday evening vaudeville program, outbid all
rivals by offering Presley the highest fee ever paid for a guest appearance. (NBC had turned
down RCA Victor's offer of Presley for his first television appearance.) Sullivan did insist,
however, on keeping the camera focussed on the singer's face and not the pelvis that was
winning the fanatical adoration of young women (and the vituperation of their parents).

As the rock-and-roll music whose viability Elvis Presley had proven continued to sell in ever-
larger quantities of recordings, the established record manufacturers increased production
of it and so too did the former "once-in-a-while indies." The goal of both the new popular-
music industry and the established firms that first began to take interest in rock was to obtain
new releases, whose fate was usually settled within three or four weeks. Some of these did
make profits, or at least retrieve initial production and promotion costs, but fewer than
100 of those released by the majors achieved best-seller status. The music-trade press reflected the real excitement, all of which was in the singles' market where rock-and-roll
predominated.

One result of the major ASCAP publishing houses' concentration on their existing catalogues
and television performances was a failure to acquire many of the new and successful rock-
and-roll songs. Young songwriters went directly to the A&R men, bypassing the publishers.
The cost of recording equipment had become more reasonable, and the songwriters could
afford to produce "demonstration" records which were submitted in place of the traditional
written-out "lead sheets." In New York City alone during 1956, some 35,000 of these
"demos" were offered to recording companies. [40] The material on such a recording that
was accepted was often placed with a company-owned publishing firm, or with a publisher
friendly to the A&R men.

By 1958, however, Richard Schickel found some sunshine behind the rock-and-roll clouds
that had, in the opinion of many, overshadowed all other music:

> . . . [there is] a slight trend away from rock'n'roll. Young singers like Johnny
> Mathis and Pat Boone, who are not primarily rock'n'rollers, have found favor
> with the kids. Some of the radio stations have been cutting back on their

rock'n'roll programming: they found they have been driving adults away with it—and adults, despite the prosperity of their children, are the people advertisers want to sell.[41]

The "Songwriters of America" vs. Rock-and-Roll: 1953-59

Such a decline in the popularity of rock-and-roll as Schickel discerned was bad news indeed to a group of songwriters based in New York and Hollywood who had gone to the law courts in a crusade for the return of "the good music of the past," for they had based their entire case on the spreading national presence of the new youth music. An anti-trust action against BMI, now licenser of most rock-and-roll music, had been initiated in November 1953 by the "Songwriters of America," a vaguely defined group of 33 song composers. The distinguished musical-theater composer, Arthur Schwartz, was key plaintiff among a veritable "Who's Who" of the musical world which also included Ira Gershwin, Gian Carlo Menotti, Samuel Barber, Virgil Thomson, Oscar Hammerstein II, and Jack Lawrence. The private suit—ASCAP was not technically involved—called for a trial by jury, with a claim of $150 million in triple damages against the defendants: BMI, NBC, CBS, ABC, Columbia Records, RCA Victor Records, and 27 private individuals. The basic charge was that an illegal combination of radio and television broadcasters, as well as the two record manufacturers, had discriminated against the plaintiffs (many of them past or present ASCAP officers or directors) and all ASCAP members by keeping their music from being recorded and played on the air. As a result, they alleged, they had suffered loss of earnings, prestige, and recognition.

Much was made, in publicity handed out at a press conference announcing the action, of its being part of a struggle to restore the "good music" that once had dominated radio programming. That music, the Songwriters of America complained, had yielded to an invasion of rock-and-roll, with its "definite tieup with juvenile delinquency." The underlying propositions appeared to be: (1) we never had rock-and-roll before BMI; (2) we never had juvenile delinquency before BMI; therefore, (3) remove BMI and you get rid of both. A BMI communication issued in 1940 was dragged out; it had referred to the withdrawal of 40% of the ASCAP catalogue in 1936 when the Warner Brothers' music interests attempted to go it alone as an alternate source of music licensing:

> Remember! The broadcasters' revolt against the music monopoly does not carry the industry into entirely uncharted territory. The industry remembers the instance of those publishers who withdrew their music in 1936. This experience taught broadcasters that they could make the air a free medium in

the field of music. It proved that the public selects its favorites from the music which it hears and does not miss what it does not hear. . . . [42]

Citing only the last twenty words of the paragraph ("the public selects . . ."), the plaintiffs labelled them an "ominous threat of suppression" on the part of BMI. They failed to mention, of course, that these words were a tidy restatement of the idea behind Tin Pan Alley's own marvelous hit-making machine with its endless exploitation of selected songs over the air.

The following two and a half years were devoted to tedious pre-trial examination of both sides; while this went on, a public-relations campaign was mounted by paid representatives of the plaintiffs, and many of their supporters as well, against the new youth music and its supposed Frankenstein monster, BMI.

In 1956 the 33 songwriter-plaintiffs and their propagandists, and many ASCAP members (5% of whose performance royalties were supporting the action), took advantage of the growing reaction against rock-and-roll music. Any disparaging reference to "the Pelvis" or rhythm-and-blues' popularity was exploited in hopes of arousing public opinion favorable to the progress of the lawsuit. A champion was found in Emanuel Celler, chairman of the House of Representatives Judiciary Committee (the very body that would sit many years later to frame articles for the impeachment of the President of the United States). The BMI case was adroitly maneuvered into complex hearings dealing with monopoly problems in regulated industries, specifically television, the major user of the sort of music for whose return to the airwaves the Songwriters of America had been campaigning. Even before any testimony was heard, Congressman Celler announced that BMI was responsible for Elvis Presley, whose "animal posturings" incited juvenile delinquency, and charged that rock-and-roll, which was "violative of all good taste," was a "natural expression" of black America's emotions and feelings. [43]

The once-and-future ASCAP president, Stanley Adams, did not refer during his appearance before the House Committee to rock-and-roll's "theme song," *Rock Around the Clock*, which was licensed by the Society. Under oath in pre-trial examinations, Adams had testified that he did not have "any personal knowledge of any act of discrimination against ASCAP music." When asked by the chairman, as an expert witness, why writers and publishers of the new music went to BMI and not ASCAP, he said it was "because they could make a fast buck," referring to the advances against earnings offered by BMI to publishers—and to songwriters as well—after 1949. [44]

After all was said and done at the hearings, the final judgment was that the matter should be referred to the Justice Department, which had been involved in the ASCAP-broadcaster-BMI situation since 1940.

Even as some people were hailing the apparent decline of rock-and-roll in 1958, the Song-writers of America returned to combat again. The new battlefield was a Senate hearing room, and the issue was a proposed amendment to the Communications Act of 1934 which would deny licenses for a broadcasting facility to any person or corporation engaged, directly or indirectly, in the business of publishing music or of manufacturing or selling musical recordings. Many of the plaintiffs in the $150 million *Schwartz vs. BMI* case were again in evidence; many of the old charges were repeated. Vance Packard, a best-selling researcher and author, and a man claimed as expert on "the manipulation of American Musical taste"—specifically in regard to "economically cheap hillbilly music . . . rock and roll . . . and a pallid young man named Elvis Presley"—complained that Buddy Holly's song *Peggy Sue* repeated the name 18 times and that *Hound Dog* had been "scribbled out in pencil on ordinary paper;" he also asserted that

> . . . rock and roll . . . was inspired by what has been called race music modified to stir the animal instinct in modern teen-agers. Its chief characteristics now are a heavy unrelenting beat and a raw, savage tone. The lyrics tend to be either nonsensical or lewd, or both. Rock and roll might best be summed up as monotony tinged with hysteria. [45]

(Packard admitted on questioning that his testimony was based on material provided by the Songwriters of America; he also said that he was being paid for his expert testimony.)

Representatives of BMI stated that, although the music it licensed dominated the country-music, rhythm-and-blues, and rock-and-roll charts, ASCAP still got 85% of all television performances and 70% of all radio performances—and three times more income from broadcasters than BMI.

After 1,237 pages of testimony and exhibits both for and against the proposed legislation, the bill failed to be voted out of committee and was effectively shelved.

The Record Industry Booms . . .

In the mid-Fifties a number of developments led to an immense boom in the record industry—tie-ins with the movie business, record clubs, the "one-stop" distributor system, the rack jobber, and the discounter. The dollar amount of records sold at list had doubled in four years; in 1958 it stood at $511 million (sales of printed music were only $30 million), as the independent labels were making inroads on the major diskeries' singles sales (which represented 59% of all units sold in stores). The new firms had learned that early and consistent plugging by a "breakout" record-spinner in Boston, Philadelphia, Detroit,

Cleveland, Chicago, or San Francisco could send a new release on its way to success. Although record buyers were interested in a greater variety of music than ever, it appeared to be a rock-and-roll world, dominated by teen-agers who purchased more of the singles offered than did any other group. While the independents' success cut in on sales of the majors' singles, at the same time their production plants were working to capacity to supply rock-and-roll and rhythm-and-blues records to the smaller firms. RCA Victor occasionally found its pressing facilities unable to handle the company's own orders; swamped with business from "left field," they sometimes even had to farm out work to rival majors' pressing plants. And the large manufacturers were optimistic about the future, believing that the record-buying habit would continue as the young people became adults and turned their interest to albums of jazz, classical, and "better" popular music. There was, in sum, "no crepe hanging over the majors," as Mike Gross wrote:

> RCA Victor, Columbia, Decca, and Capitol are running way ahead in the sales take. They've gotten their share of the pop pull and have been cleaning up with the packaged product. It's this mushrooming field, in fact, that tradesters figure may be the undoing of a lot of indie operations.

> After having kicked up some coin with the pop clicks, quite a few of the indies have been going after larger game in the album field. It's this splurge into the packaged food markets that's making the indies nervous. At the $3.95 tap for a pop LP, the profit margin is pretty slim considering the rising costs in recording, art work, promotion, etc. The majors get by on sales volume, while indies, with a small LP catalog to work with, have found it tough sledding to pull their line into the profit column.

> They're not running scared yet, however, and are holding the fort despite some nifty buyout offers. They figure the market's big and getting bigger and that they'll eventually get their share.

> And with the growing interest of motion picture companies in the disk biz, the indies can afford to sit it out until some irresistible offer comes up. . . . The film companies want into the record business for more than just pic tie-in reasons. They realize it's a booming business and they want a share. [46]

The bright future of the record business and its relationship to the motion-picture industry had been outlined in a *Variety* editorial (12 February 1958) pointing out that "it was time to grow up." The profit of $1.3 million realized by Loew's Inc., one of the major filmmakers, had come not from production and distribution of motion pictures but from the ownership of a record company, three music publishing houses, and a New York radio station.

The major record labels had been expanding their distribution chains for several years, beginning with the formation of the Columbia Record Club in 1955. The year before, Goddard Lieberson, then executive vice president of Columbia Records, had often asserted his feeling that the record business was "still tiny . . . like the book trade—low volume and inefficient distribution." To protect an investment in albums made during the previous dozen years but no longer being promoted, as well as to counter falling sales of "good old music," Columbia added direct-mail service to its distribution system. With this the company tapped a potential market of several million people, mostly over 35 years old, who would otherwise have been lost. By 1959, witnessing Columbia's success with a million-member club grossing $30 million annually, RCA and Capitol began clubs of their own.

There had been an addition to the sales process, one which the manufacturers could not really control: the "one-stop" distributor who handled all labels, for sale to jukebox operators (who could thereby buy all the singles they needed from a central source) and to small, unaffiliated record retailers who bought about 20% of their singles and LPs from them. In the late 1950s, the one-stops were distributing more than one-half of all singles.

Another newcomer to the distribution process was the "rack jobber," whose self-service metal racks were located near cash registers in drugstores, supermarkets, and variety stores—especially chain stores. Purchasing directly from the manufacturer, rack jobbers accounted for about 30% of all LP unit sales at retail in the early 1960s, and they finally destroyed the old-fashioned "mom and pop" retail stores that had been the industry's first link to the public. The "racks" also distributed low-price, economy and budget (99 cent) LPs and selected singles, thus helping to maintain the popularity of such middle-of-the-road music as the Mitch Miller choral selections, and songs from the Broadway musicals and their filmed Hollywood versions. The rackers also cleared company storage vaults of material by performers once popular but now slipping, as well as re-issues of earlier best-selling items, personality packages, and children's records.

Record companies also came to own many of the largest discount stores, which Sam Goody of New York pioneered in the early 1950s. These were (and are) full-service retail shops that stocked most labels as well as electronic equipment and musical instruments and supplies. With a 100% return-to-manufacturer privilege, Goody found that even though he cut list prices by 30%, he had about the same in profit after discount and could double or triple his income through an increased volume of sales. With dramatic newspaper and radio advertising, discounters multiplied in the major markets and opened branches in the suburban shopping centers that had mushroomed after the downtown areas of large cities became regarded as unsafe because of racial and social problems. Another important factor in the discounters' success was "trans-shipping." In this practice, record distributors, whose allocation of new releases was based on past sales, maintained quotas by trans-shipping overstocks to discounters, usually at a very low price. Advertising these as "loss leaders," the discount-record stores attracted customers who left with other records as well.

. . . The Payola Scandal Looms

Many conservative AM broadcasters, who daily faced a barrage of anti-rock-and-roll propaganda that was aimed not only at them but at advertisers, the press, the pulpit, and parents, grew uneasy. Fearing that payola revelations might affect their operations, as early as 1953 some station owners in Middle America sought to curb pay-for-play and to control music selection, and looked for program formats that would do both. They hoped also to find a formula that would give them some individuality among the hundreds of stations that, like them, relied on a music-and-news policy. Some thought they saw an answer in the great popularity of a few selections among the 40 tunes available on the standard jukebox; others recalled the concentration on ten top tunes with which *Your Hit Parade* had held radio audiences during the 1930s and '40s, and now was holding television audiences. Thus arose "Top 40" programming, which, employing a small body of songs based on reports of national and local popularity and chosen by management, took the place of disc-jockey-selected music and dominated AM broadcasting by the late 1950s. Unlike the print medium or television, Top 40 programs demanded little concentration on the part of their audiences, 50% of which were outside the home, many in the 40 million automobiles that by 1960 were equipped with radios, or were listening to a transistor set (the number of which was impossible to measure).

As a business which thrives on imitation of a successful idea, radio took to the new format with great joy. Top 40 with its "purified pop" served to cleanse the image of its born-again practitioners, who were still recovering from a close call (the Washington hearings in mid-1958 which had threatened profit losses with an amendment of the Communications Act that would have put an end to pre-recorded musical programming as well as the studio-produced advertising that was heavily dependent on recorded sound and popular music). Back of their enthusiasm, too, was a sense of relief that, like other fads, rock-and-roll finally appeared to be going the way of flagpole-sitting and goldfish-swallowing. But, as David T. MacFarland wrote, the Top 40 format,

> . . . coupled with teen-agers' increased spending power, encouraged a renaissance in the phonograph industry that would eventually see the new 45 replaced by sale of LPs. New music and novel promotion—the same two elements that propelled Top 40 to be the most imitated radio formula in the world—also were two factors behind the success of Elvis Presley, Dick Clark, Motown, the Beatles, folk-rock, progressive rock . . . and much more . . . and it all came from Middle America.[47]

Network television, long the bastion of Tin Pan Alley's "good music" and secure in the protection of its immense popularity, finally dared to embrace young America with a kind of rock-and-roll, first seen nationally in 1957 and programmed daily after school, in the form of ABC-TV's show *American Bandstand*. The compère of this La Scala of pop music was Dick Clark, the most successful and influential television disc jockey of all time. By 1960, *American Bandstand* was responsible for $12 million worth of air-time sales and Clearasil had become a household word.

In that same year Congress entered into a payola probe, with hearings beginning in April. The probe had been instigated by the songwriter-plaintiffs in the earlier anti-trust action against BMI and other defendants charging a national conspiracy to foist "bad music and rock-and-roll" on the American public. That suit had finally come to trial in 1959, but because ASCAP, agent by assignment for the songwriters' performing rights, was not part of the action, the damage claims were removed by order of the presiding judge. [48] Those expected millions now never to be gained, the Songwriters of America turned again to Washington for a public forum in which to air their grievances. In late 1959, persuaded that the issue should be investigated, the House Interstate and Foreign Commerce Legislative Oversight Committee, having concluded a first set of hearings on television-show rigging and alleged payola to performers, was now ready to announce which aspect of broadcasting it would look into next. Late one afternoon, just as the chairman was about to call a recess, a representative of the Songwriters of America strode down the aisle bearing documents he proclaimed would clearly prove the conspiracy of disc jockeys, broadcasters, and record manufacturers to suppress genuine talent. Platter-spinners and record-promotion men were subpoenaed from around the country. One invited witness, Paul Ackerman (music editor of *Billboard*), provided both a historical perspective and an insider's point of view of the music business and its long involvement with pay-for-play.

> Much of the investigation of the music industry has centered around the so-called singles record business, which is a very small part of the total record business. The singles business is a declining one and in December [1959] represented only 20% of the industry's dollar volume [of over $40 million]. . . . Long-play records currently account for approximately 80% of the total dollar volume. [49]

It was, Ackerman stated, the very abundance of "product," resulting from the great expansion during the previous twenty years of music-publishing firms, songwriters, record companies, and radio stations, that had in effect removed control of hit-making from Tin Pan Alley and put it into the hands of local radio programmers and record manufacturers. A major-market station or disc jockey received more than 1,000 LPs annually and over 5,000 45-r.p.m. singles, representing a total of at least 20,000 individual selections. Competition for exposure of this surfeit to mass audiences had become extreme, and with it had come all types of payola.

The Congressmen were determined to concentrate only on payola for rock-and-roll, not on that for performances of the "good music of the past." A random remark of one witness that he had been paid to favor one label's version of a Tchaikovsky symphony over another's elicited the response that the Committee was not interested in anything but pay-for-play in relation to "bad" music. Veterans in the press gallery noted that 1960 was an election year, with House members seeking to return to their places of power, and that rock-and-roll fans didn't vote; purchasers of the majority of record releases, middle-of-the-road music, did.

The hearings adduced findings from 335 jockeys that they had been paid $263,245 as "consultant fees" in the recent past. Virtually all of them were in major "breakout" cities (New York, Detroit, Cleveland, Boston, and Philadelphia); their influence was great on small-fry dee jays, who, like the industry employing them, had a tendency to follow the leader. One of the witnesses who admitted that he had taken cash and other gifts protested that he had in no way been influenced, that he was given the money by record companies in the hope that "something good would happen." Another said that payola was "the American way." It appeared to some cynical spectators that he was indeed correct, for testimony already heard had led to the resignation of the FCC Chairman, another Commissioner, and an assistant to the President of the United States (whose pressures on the Federal Trade Commission brought about his downfall). However, President Eisenhower, who commented on disc-jockey payola, did not equate it with pay for political favor, even though it had involved a number of his own appointees.

The upshot of the Committee hearings was that Congress amended the Communications Act of 1934 and outlawed all pay-for-play, with a year's jail term and a maximum fine of $10,000 for convicted offenders. History's appraisal of the deliberations may have been best written by Bernard Schwartz, who served as counsel but was dismissed in an argument over the direction in which the hearings were going (namely, a certain reluctance to investigate political payola). Before the disc-jockey hearings were announced in late 1959 he wrote:

> For a word that is not even contained in Webster, "payola" has certainly gone far in recent weeks toward becoming one of the most familiar words in the American vocabulary. The current probe of the Harris Committee into payola and other dubious usages in TV has made the nation fully aware of all the ramifications involved in these sordid practices.

What the country does not realize, however, is that improprieties other than those committed by Charles Van Doren, Alan Freed, et al.—what may aptly be described as the "real payola"—have thus far remained buried in the Harris Committee's files.

Those aware of the material involved know that we are sadly deceiving ourselves to believe that the Congressmen carried out anything like the really thorough investigation of the federal agencies that is so urgently needed. [50]

Music, Radio and the Record Business: 1961-1975

The four major record manufacturers enjoyed 50% of the LP market in the early 1960s and shipped to members of their record clubs 24% of all discs sold. Some leading independents had already been purchased by corporations in the entertainment business as well as outside it. The motion-picture industry had been among the first to recognize the potential profits of the business, and others were beginning to become aware of them. Many elements of the five conglomerates that were to control over 82% of the 1982 recordings market were already in place; only Atlantic and Elektra still functioned as independents. The European conglomerate Polygram was yet to be created, as was its most profitable American partner, RSO, the Robert Stigwood Organization, which helped Polygram sell more than $1 billion worth of recorded music in their first year of joint operation (1978).

The general business recession facing John F. Kennedy when he became President in 1961 gradually subsided, but the old excitement stemming from the cross-pollenization of country music with rhythm-and-blues appeared to be gone forever. The "Philadelphia schlock" promoted by Dick Clark over *American Bandstand* (which emanated from the Quaker City and featured locally produced non-singing "teen idols") had thrust rock-and-roll into a "treacle period" from which it had not yet extricated itself: the four top-selling popular LPs of the year were from Hollywood film and Broadway musical scores; Lawrence Welk was number 11 on the top rock-and-roll singles chart. Elvis Presley had returned from the army to shore up RCA Victor's profits with albums of songs from his Hollywood movies, eventually thirty of them, for each of which he usually received $1 million. His songs now were generally a sanitized popular music, though still labeled rock-and-roll; but this former target of a Congressional Committee chairman's abuse had been "depelvisated" by his film producers, and his A&R men almost always turned Elvis away from "country's rock and r&b roll" into the middle of the road, where he stayed until his death, except for a brief period in the late 1960s.

In 1963, Capitol Record executives were not particularly enthusiastic about a new British vocal group, the Beatles. Only after their recently acquired proprietors, Electrical and Musical Industries, Ltd. (EMI), a British holding company, persuaded them otherwise did the American company spend $50,000 to promote the group's anticipated appearance in the USA. The Beatles arrived in New York in early 1964 to triumphant receptions which reminded the industry of the days when Frank Sinatra, and later Elvis Presley, had "turned on" young American women. Before the year ended, the Fab Four had six Number One singles and were beginning the long string of Number One LPs which accounted for the major portion of the 150 million dollars' worth of recorded music they sold in the next several years.

It was during this period that the country's first successful black-owned independent recording and music publishing empire, Motown of Detroit, came of age. The firm's first and still sole stockholder, Berry Gordy, had produced and sold master recordings of polite rhythm-and-blues singles to New York major labels during the late 1950s. Then he went out on his own. Financed with money borrowed from his family, plus an advance from BMI for on-the-road promotion, Gordy started with a version of rhythm-and-blues with a gospel sound, for sale to both black and white middle-class buyers of mainstream popular music. In late 1963, when Motown dropped gospel-music tambourines from its recordings, *Billboard* (coincidentally) abandoned its rhythm-and-blues LP charts: commercial black music had finally crossed over into Top 40 land. The growth of white concern for black capitalism a few years later made possible Motown's transition into Motown Industries of Los Angeles, a show-business conglomerate which grossed over $90 million in 1981 (when it no longer ranked among the top six—CBS, Capitol, MCA, Polygram, RCA, and Warner Communications—that controlled over 85% of the US market).

Virtually single-handed, if not overnight, the Beatles changed the American record manufacturers' long-held attitudes toward the making and selling of hit records. They introduced the performer/songwriter who selected or wrote his own material and then, until he mastered the craft, produced it with some technical assistance from a company employee or independent producer. The Beatles stretched the boundaries of popular-song lyrics by dealing with controversial subjects appealing to the below-25-year-olds, who made them kings of the heap. After 700 hours of studio time, an unheard-of amount to devote to a single album, and with the music enhanced by the use of multi-track recording, electronic sounds, and other effects never before used for the purpose, the Beatles delivered the first successful "concept album," *Sgt. Pepper's Lonely Hearts Club Band*. Perhaps most significantly, the four young Britons rekindled record manufacturers' interest in recording and merchandising rock music, and stimulated so frantic a search for talent that the major companies willingly surrendered artistic control over repertoire and product in order to sign any and every promising talent. The most financially successful American music yet offered was built around a rhythm-and-blues beat, and it raised record sales to over the $1 billion mark in 1967. Its audience was the under-25 age group that formed roughly half of the total population, and they soon abandoned the 45-r.p.m. single in favor of the LP album, which happened to be more profitable to the manufacturers. The repeal in 1965 of a federal excise tax of 10% on the first billing price of all records sold, whether of native manufacture or foreign, had already increased profits. The LP was now "where the money was," and the major labels concentrated their promotion and merchandising efforts on its sale. Another manipulated increase of profits followed in 1969, when the average number of selections on a 12-inch LP was reduced from between 12 and 16 to a standard of 10; this automatically cut mechanical royalties to songwriters and publishers. During this period, when sales rose from $698 million in 1963 to $2 billion in 1973 at a steady growth rate of 10%, a new breed of conglomerator found the purchase of record-manufacturing facilities irresistible, as LP prices, which accounted for 80% of all sales, rose from $4.98 in 1967 to $7.97 seven years later. The industry's continuing profit growth overrode the great financial losses that followed some major errors of judgment. There appeared to be no way for corporate income to go but up, as technology increased the opportunities for promotion.

During the early 1960s, half of all AM stations were located in one- and two-market coverage areas, serving their listeners a mixed musical fare, usually from singles, that occupied more than 80% of all air time. There were as many as 40 stations in a major market; they used various programming formats, changing them frequently in the hope that audiences would grow and that consequently advertising sales would too. In 1963 more than 6,000 singles and approximately 4,000 LPs were released. However, only one of every five singles sent to broadcasters by the majors was played more than one time, and selections from only two of every three LPs. Three hundred of the new singles were regarded as hits, but only 26 of them sold more than a million copies.

As the stations that had first dared to program rock-and-roll changed formats under the pressure of successful Top 40 format competitors, teen-agers and young adults began to look elsewhere for new music; after 1965 they discovered what they wanted on the FM spectrum. Frequency-modulation (FM) broadcasting—an industry orphan before World War II, when television staked a claim to its original frequency band—came into its own shortly after the Beatles' initial success, when the FCC prohibited duplication of AM programming in markets with more than 100,000 potential listeners. Many station-owners turned to separate and divided operations, keeping the most lucrative programming on AM and leaving FM to find its own way. That way proved to be the use of the LP album with its longer cuts and more adventurous popular rock music—another result of the Beatles' striking alteration of the status quo: once the four British superstars had produced the album of the decade, *Sgt. Pepper*, the major labels quickly increased all LP output by 10% and reduced manufacture of singles by 21%.

The music of "underground" FM's first several years on the air was chosen by its own "laid-back" dee jays. However, cautious station owners, looking for profits following the intro-duction of FM stereo, resorted to ever-narrowing playlists of progressive rock's newest forms as well as album cuts of less-advanced popular music. Abandoning the pre-teens and teen-agers to the AM stations, and buttressed by stereo's improved sound, from the late 1960s rock-album-oriented FM was pinpointed toward a market aged 18 to 34.

In late 1964, as BMI's share of the top song-hits had risen to 80% (in 1948 it had been 10%, in 1958 57%), an anti-trust suit was filed by the Justice Department against the broadcaster-owners of BMI stock, their number reduced to 517 through the sale back to BMI of the holdings in the organization by the three networks and a number of independent station owners. [51] This suit was terminated two years later with a consent decree that permitted broadcasters to retain their ownership of BMI stock but prohibited BMI from publication of music, from making recordings or engaging in commercial distribution of recordings or printed music, and from "coercing performance or recording" of music.

The year 1966 also marked a number of major turning points in the music-publishing world. For one thing, the Music Publishers Protective Association, which had replaced the nineteenth-century Board of Music Trade monopolistic trust, changed its name and its general attitude toward competitor non-members. The "new" National Music Publishers Association purged its one-time self-perpetuating board of directors and enlarged it to include representatives of the country-music, rhythm-and-blues, and rock-and-roll firms established after the 1941 "music war." Under enlightened officers, directors, and managing executives of NMPA, former antagonisms between songwriters and song-publishers abated. The NMPA and AGAC (The American Guild of Authors and Composers, formerly the Songwriters Protective Asso-ciation [SPA]), began to cooperate in statesmanlike fashion and joined forces in the struggle to revise the 1909 copyright act and in confronting other mutual problems. After ten years of harmony, in 1975 AGAC's president could say about the publishers represented by the NMPA:

> We view [them] as our partners in a sense that is best described by the word
> "symbiosis." It is true that a publisher's work may not begin until our work
> is complete, but, in a large sense, our work is not complete until they exercise
> their functions properly as publishers.[52]

The Beatles' work of the mid-1960s also affected the traditional relationship between writer and publisher. Following an example set by the group, rock songwriter-performers (whose financial success often required the full-time services of lawyers, accountants, and managers) began to insist on retention of all copyrights. However, shares in their music, which now appeared chiefly on plastic (with sales of recordings ten times greater than those of printed music), were, and continue to be, assigned to large publishing companies. These serve as agent and partner: they administer various property rights, promote the music after initial demand for it has abated, represent writers in the multi-billion-dollar international business, and perform other traditional music-publisher functions. As a result of this sharing of copyrights, it is not unusual to see four or more publishers listed as owners of songs, the majority being those members of the group who had written/recorded them.

In 1966, too, ASCAP began to offer money in advance of royalties to songwriters and publishers, a BMI practice about which the Society's spokesmen had long complained, both publicly and in representations to the United States government. Among those benefiting from the change in ASCAP policy were many whose music had once been excoriated by the Society's leaders. By the early 1980s, under Hal David, its songwriter-president who won renown by writing and producing recorded music intended essentially for the youth market, ASCAP had become a vigorous competitor in all fields of music. The world's financially most successful licensing organization, ASCAP effectively displaced the long-held domination by BMI, the world's *largest* licensing organization, over the Hot 100, country, soul, gospel, rock and other charts. As Lucia S. Schultz has written:

> " . . . there is no question that competition has been good to ASCAP. The changes in ASCAP practices, forced by the presence of BMI, have only benefited the Society's members. . . ."[53]

Government intervention, too, resulting in several amendments of the ASCAP consent decree of 1941, has contributed to a distribution-of-income system that offers writers a choice between a full current performance base and one in which availability and seniority are also taken into consideration. Seventy percent of the publisher distribution is based on current performances, and the balance on the availability of "recognized works." BMI makes all payments to writers and publishers on an equal basis, for current performances only, after assigning weighted credit values to different types of music and music uses. Combined distribution by the three major licensing bodies (the third being SESAC, Inc., founded in 1930) is fast approaching $300 million annually. The obligation to pay *in order to play* has created the largest single source of income to writers and publishers, larger than the $122 million in mechanical royalties paid in 1979, and larger than the royalties in that year from an estimated gross sales of $260 million worth of printed music.

There is a growing danger, however, that the performing-rights income may decline significantly. There have been a number of suits against ASCAP and BMI, singly and together, instituted by music users, charging monopolistic practices and other violations of anti-trust laws. The most important of these, *Buffalo vs. ASCAP, BMI*, initiated on 28 November 1978 as a class action on behalf of approximately 750 independent television stations, challenges the traditional blanket licensing of music, and if won by the plaintiffs can result in a reduction by about 30% of income to writers and publishers. Those who remember 1940, when the Justice Department's Antitrust Division believed that the Sherman Act superseded laws governing copyright in certain instances, facilitating the formation of BMI, wonder whether that same philosophy might resurface in the courtroom now, four decades later. However, the issue may be resolved in the marketplace long before it reaches the Supreme Court, as inevitably it will and must.

From Sheet Music's Print to the LP's Plastic

Many details of the growth and practices of the recording industry during the late 1960s and the '70s appear in testimony offered to Congressional bodies and government tribunals, either for or against the removal of compulsory licensing and/or a change in the royalty of 2 cents per record. There was little question that compulsory licensing would be abolished, and an increase in the royalty payment became the matter of most interest. The new act carried provision that the royalty be initially increased to 2-3/4 cents per selection or 1/2 cent per minute (or fraction thereof) of playing time, whichever is larger. The review of the mechanical royalty rates was placed into the hands of the new Copyright Royalty Tribunal (CRT), and in December 1980 it increased the rate to 4 cents a selection or 3/4 cents per minute, whichever is larger. CRT will continue to adjust the rate in steps: on 1 January 1983, to 4-1/4 cents or 0.8 cents a minute: 1 July 1984, to 4-1/2 cents or 0.85 cents; and finally on 1 January 1986, the rate will be 5 cents or 0.9 cents per minute, in all cases whichever is larger.

During the course of congressional hearings affecting copyright revision in 1975, Stanley M. Gortikov, president of the Recording Industry Association of America, Inc. (RIAA), told the committee in testimony, some of which was little noted at the time, that the large manufacturers he represented had in effect taken over control of the marvelous hit-making machine:

> Once music publishers performed many more creative promotional marketing functions for their 2 cents than most do today for 20 to 24 cents [referring to the total fees from an LP]. Their function today is heavily administrative and clerical; they are largely service entities, conduits for the processing of income and paper transactions. They don't promote as they used to. They

don't employ field representatives as they used to. They don't create demand as they used to. These functions have necessarily been taken over by the recording companies.[54]

The RIAA president omitted to mention that although the industry he represented had assumed control of all the hit-making procedures in the ancient machine created by Tin Pan Alley, its rate of success in creating hits had been little better than that of the publishers. John D. Glover, director of the Cambridge Research Institute, appeared during the same hearings to provide statistical testimony in support of Gortikov's statement. He said, in part:

> When I was here before [in 1965] we showed you at that time on popular LPs they took about 7,800 copies before you got your breakeven point. That figure is now up to 61,000; 61,000 copies before you got your original investment back. In 1963, in fact, 61 percent of the records released did not, in fact, get their cost back, let alone make any money. And that figure has now risen to 77 percent. So, you have a 77 percent chance of not getting your money back, let alone making any money.[55]

With its control of the hit-making machine, the record industry had become involved with the procedure's inherent flaws and excesses in the promotion and exploitation by constant repetition of pre-selected newly recorded popular music. A writer, in a spring 1979 issue of *Fortune*, reported:

> Record-industry executives maintain, not surprisingly, that payola is a thing of the past. Federal investigators familiar with the seamier side of the business agree, at least in the sense that the record companies are putting considerable distance between their organizations and the putative dispensing of cash for radio play. Suspicions these days—without much solid evidence—center on free-lance promotion men. . . .

> Promotion [program] directors and disc jockeys are increasingly being wooed with a more respectable business weapon—information. Armed with the numbers on sales and accounts of radio reception in other towns, the promoters travel their territories—liberally dispensing free concert tickets, talking up new releases, and explaining why certain records are just what a particular radio audience is longing for. . . .

> . . . Among the tarnished verities is the old industry aphorism "It's what's in the grooves that counts." It still does count, of course, but no one wins the platinum derby these days without a lot of money and marketing clout.[56]

Between the time Elvis Presley checked his *Hound Dog* into *Heartbreak Hotel* and the super-star's death, annual gross sales of recordings at list climbed from $400 million to $4.1 billion. Presley's passing in 1977 brought about a wave of album-buying on the part of loyal fans as well as others to whom his career had assumed mythic proportions. This was followed by a new, cheap-to-produce disco-record craze, out of which came two all-time bestselling LPs derived from film scores, *Saturday Night Fever* and *Grease*. Their sales played an important part in a $1.6 billion gross by the then-little-known Polygram firm, the first to break the $1 billion sales mark. "Cross-over marketing" (using movies and their music to sell each other), as the manufacturers labeled it, was an old Tin Pan Alley principle, but the Polygram promotion applied it to greater effect than ever known before; Polygram's success made more dramatic than ever the relationship between popular-song exploitation and film success, an important element of the hit-making process in the 1930s and wartime 1940s, when films accounted for about 30% of each year's hit songs, Broadway supplying about 15%.[57]

Bidding for the superstars, an intermittent industry practice following the Beatles' success in the mid-1960s, brought about battles between the major labels in 1978. The hoped-for hit-makers were secured by contracts involving unheard-of advances, guarantees, and royalty rates. Paul Simon was offered—and signed—a contract guaranteeing him more than $13 million so that he would leave Columbia, the major label for which he first recorded, to go with Warner Brothers. The former Beatle, Paul McCartney, left his original American label (Capitol) after signing a contract with Columbia guaranteeing $2 million on only the American and Canadian rights to each LP; after that was earned, a royalty of 22% on additional sales would begin. To sweeten the original deal, songwriter and music publisher Frank Loesser's catalogue of popular and Broadway music, owned by CBS and valued at several million dollars, was added to the negotiations. Under these and similar new contracts, sales of at least more than a quarter-million units were necessary before one penny of profit was realized.

In anticipation of the continuing sales growth that other similar arrangements were also expected to provide, new record-pressing plants were erected, and millions of discs by the super-talents were pressed, the price of each raised to $8.98. The 100% return privilege offered to record retailers on all unsold product boomeranged when millions of LPs were returned, to be credited against *new* product. To add to the confusion, pirate copies also flooded the market and inflated the returns; they were the latest manifestation of an age-old problem for mass producers of music.

To save money needed to acquire the dreamed-of blockbusting superstar hits, talented performers, but ones who could not be expected to produce similar sales figures, were dropped from company rosters. Disco began to fizzle out, and higher gasoline prices took their toll of record buyers' assets. Rising oil prices increased the cost of vinyl, of which records and tapes are made. The superstars failed to deliver best-selling new product, and a half-billion-dollar loss followed, rather than the anticipated 10% growth rate.

Today, the paucity of "hot new product" keeps hit albums on the charts 25% longer than a few years ago. The decision in May 1982 by WABC, New York City's premier rock station, to switch from a Top-40 formula to a talk-and-news format led to the prediction that what the music business has acknowledged to be the "best sales and exploitation medium it has ever known" will eventually disappear from other stations and in time, from AM radio. Music on the air has become predominantly an FM business. More than half of all Americans hear their music on FM, with its stereo made even more accessible by SONY's "Walkman" portable cassette-deck/radio-receiver and its imitators. Knowledgeable radio men predict that although stereo AM may be coming soon, most AM stations will abandon music programming entirely and leave it all to FM. Such an eventuality will, of course, cut even more seriously into performing-rights income.

In pursuit of a profitable bottom line, major disc-makers have abandoned risk-taking and have resorted to an essentially conservative product many of them privately call "bland" or even "boring." They point, as one reason, to the demands of changing Top-40 policies. John Sebastian, one of that formula's Doctor Strangeloves, has suggested that AM must depend on "passive research" to learn not "what listeners actually like but what they find least offensive."[58] In essence, that has always been the course pursued by the major manufacturers when faced with such changes in music as the advent of rock-and-roll.

In the process of cutting costs by deleting merchandise whose shelf life has been found wanting by the manufactuers' computerized analysis, "unprofitable" examples of recorded creativity in all fields of contemporary music disappear from circulation. Contemporary concert music has been virtually abandoned by the major companies to six German-owned labels (which already record half of *all* classical music). American composers have found a new but small outlet for their work on the plastic that now permits the largest distribution, produced by new independent record makers. As once did rhythm-and-blues audiences, Americans seeking new and innovative popular music, as well as those who love traditional forms, must look to such small new competitors of the established order.

The critics of the major manufacturers complain about the indiscriminate corner-cutting that produces records full of pops and other surface noise (many feel that records pressed twenty years ago sound better); discs warped by overly tight shrink-wrapping that makes an extra penny's profit on each sale; records made from recycled vinylite, resulting in quality far below that of foreign competitors. The public complains about increasing prices—not caring, of course, that they are effected to counter falling profits. (Within the single year of 1981, the average price of an LP album rose 61 cents, to $7.75; singles 7 cents, to $1.67; pre-recorded cassettes 57 cents, to $7.69.)

Things to Come? 1982

In 1975, seeking to demonstrate that the industry he serves expanded its output to the benefit of songwriters and publishers, thus making any increase in record royalties unnecessary, Stanley M. Gortikov, the RIAA president, told a Congressional committee that " . . . the ingenuity and risk capital of recording and equipment companies developed the 8-track cartridge and cassette. These created an entirely new additional market—about 20% of total sales—each earning 20 to 24 cents for the publisher and composer."[59] Beginning in the late 1960s all of the major manufacturers carried a line of pre-recorded cassettes, as well as blank cassettes, and advertised both in the trade and consumer press. Buyers liked cassettes because of their ease of handling, durability, and reasonably good sound quality (at that time inferior to that of discs). Sales of pre-recorded tapes (basically cassettes) rose from $478 million in 1970 to $1.06 billion in 1977; in the same period blank cassette sales rose from $18 million to $249 million,[60] and were expected to total $798.9 million in 1982. [61]

Today, Pygmalion cries publicly because of the uses to which his Galatea is being put by the home-tapers of pre-recorded music, both from recordings and off-the-air. Much the same situation faced the future of Thomas Edison's pre-recorded cylinders, but the institution of controlled production and distribution of blank cylinders as well as new technology put an end to surreptitious recordings of cylinders by competitors and in the home.

As with nuclear energy, modern recording technology has finally surpassed the record industry's ability to control it. Easy accessibility to blank cassettes permits home recording of copyrighted music. The major losers appear to be the record manufacturers, which face a multi-billion-dollar drop in annual sales of pre-recorded music. According to one survey conducted by Warner Communications,[62] taping in the home displaces an estimated $2.85 billion in annual potential pre-recorded sales. Home taping is not confined, as one might have thought, to economy-minded teenagers. 50% of all home taping is done by 20-to-34-year-olds, and 19% is done by those even older. Overall, adults account for 88% of all albums and 70% of all singles that are home-taped. On the other hand, a study made for the Electronics Industry Association, a trade group representing manufacturers of blank audio and video cassettes and hardware, found that 52% of all tapes made by 1,018 respondents to telephone interviews were not related to music but, ostensibly, to video programs and other sources.[63] Both studies found that taping exists and is growing, half of it from borrowed LPs and off-the-air. Both cited many of the same reasons for home taping of music: the longer playing time (as opposed to discs) and the easy handling and storage of cassettes; unavailability of the music because of its deletion from active catalogues; "stores make it hard to buy pre-recorded tapes"; "so I don't have to buy it"; and the creation of programs of their own selection for the tapers' use in their homes and automobiles, and on private stereo players such as the "Walkman."

None of this should have come as a surprise to the record manufacturers or the music publishers. As long ago as 1969, a vice president of marketing at RCA cited an independently conducted survey of consumers which found that 80% of reel-to-reel tape-machine owners taped radio and television programs and 44% of them taped records—most of them borrowed. Stereo cassettes and equipment were then not yet available in sufficient quantity to provide any meaningful statistics, but those who owned monophonic portable machines were taping AM/FM radio, and 27% of those surveyed were making copies of recorded music. [64]

The continuing loss from home taping now threatens the existence of American songwriters and publishers. The two already depend more or less on the pleasure of record manufacturers, who have the power to choose their music or not, record it or not, promote it or not, and if recorded, withdraw it completely from public access when it does not sell a fixed quota. Unless Congress passes legislation (which has in fact been proposed) to provide a royalty to songwriters, composers, and publishers while legalizing non-profit home taping, and unless Congress imposes compulsory licensing and royalties on the manufacturers and importers of home-recording materials—or some other way of compensating the copyright owners for the use of their material, through collection and distribution means still to be determined—the process of mass distribution of music, which has already gone from print to plastic, will add piracy to the plastic.

"Pac-Man" and his tribe are also lurking in the wings and are already affecting the sale of all music. In 1982 the sales of video games took $1.7 billion out of the personal entertainment market, siphoning money not only from the record industry but the songwriter and the music publisher as well. That figure is expected to increase to $3 billion in 1984, an amount just a little less than Americans currently spend at the movie theater box-office, and one that threatens to increase rapidly as the present 10% penetration of television households by the home video-game industry rises to the 50% saturation believed by the industry to be inevitable. Raymond Kassar, chairman of *Atari*, a leading video-game manufacturer owned by Warner Communications, believes that "the maturity level of video games will be beyond anyone's wildest dreams." [65] The future will not be the same for songwriters and publishers unless federal legislation strengthens and expands protection of the intellectual property that is music.

NOTES

(Figures regarding sales of printed music, manufacture of pianos, player pianos, music rolls, phonographs, records, and cylinders, copyright registrations, as well as others germane to music-business economics, are taken from Department of Commerce and Census of Manufactures reports issued from the 1890s to the early 1940s. Trade-paper accounts figure in those of printed music sales from then until 1958, when the Music Publishers Protective Association (MPPA, called after 1966 National Music Publishers Association, or NMPA) began to issue annual reports. The figures for annual sales of phonograph records in the period following World War I to the present are taken from statistics prepared by the Recording Industry Association of America, Inc. (RIAA). However, I relied on figures released by John Griffin, executive secretary of RIAA, on 7 October 1958, for the years 1921-1954; these were, as he described them, "based on best guesses, trade papers, excise tax records, etc." In many cases they differ from the later RIAA figures, but I choose them because they were arrived at by people active in the recording industry during the time.)

[1] Barbara Ringer, *Two Hundred Years of Copyright in America* (mimeographed; Washington, DC, 1976), p. 16.

[2] From Testimony by F.L. Dyer, attorney for the Edison Manufacturing Company, in *Hearings Before the Committee on Patents, March 26-28, 1908* (Washington, DC: Government Printing Office, 1908), p. 284.

> ... The figures that have been submitted to the chairmen of these two committees show that notwithstanding the fact that there has been no attempt on the part of the [piano-roll and phonograph-recording] manufacturers to advance one interest as against another, the amount of foreign music used by them is about 70 per cent, and American music is about 30 per cent. ... This shows the natural demand of the American people. ... The manufacturers have made no effort to force upon the public foreign music to the exclusion of domestic music, because one is as free for use as the other, but the people themselves, having the opportunity of taking either, demand 70 per cent of the foreign music and only 30 per cent of the American music.

[3]Coleman Elliot, *The Oliver Ditson Company—The Story of Its Origin and Development* (unpaged and undated, but certainly post-1891; copy in the Music Research Division, New York Public Library at Lincoln Center).

[4]*Ibid.*

[5]Isidore Witmark and Isaac Goldberg, *From Ragtime to Swingtime* (New York: Leo Furman, Inc., 1939), p. 114.

[6]*Historical Statistics of the United States, Bicentennial Edition* (Washington, DC: Government Printing Office, 1975), pp. 956-7.

[7]*Census of Manufactures* (Washington, DC; Department of Commerce, 1909).

[8]Nathan Burkan, counsel for Music Publishers Association of the United States, *Hearings Before the Committees on Patents, 1908*, pp. 223-35.

[9]In 1904, when $4 million of sheet music was sold and piano sales neared the $5 million mark, the phonograph-manufacturing and recording business grossed $10 million from all its products. David Giovannoni, "The Phonograph as a Mass Entertainment Medium" (M.A. thesis, University of Wisconsin-Madison, 1980), pp. 96-97, estimates that 817,000 machines in home use in that year represented a 4.6% saturation of 17.9 million households, or 1 machine to every 22 homes; five years later, over 26 million discs and cylinders were produced annually to feed them.

[10]*Variety,* 29 February 1956, p. 1.

[11]*Ibid.*

[12]Abel Green and Joe Laurie, Jr., *Show Biz from Vaude to Video* (New York: Henry Holt & Co., 1951), p. 316.

[13]*Ibid.*

[14]*Ibid.*, p. 317.

[15]*Decisions of the United States Courts Involving Copyright 1914-1917,* Bulletin No. 18 (Washington, DC: U.S. Copyright Office, 1918), pp. 49-52.

[16]"5,000,000 Songs," *Fortune,* January 1933, pp. 27ff.

[17]*Broadcasting,* 18 June 1938, p. 18.

[18]*Variety,* 3 April 1940, p. 43.

[19]Duncan MacDougald, Jr., "The Popular Music Industry," in Paul F. Lazarsfeld and Frank Stanton, *Radio Research 1941* (New York: Duell, Sloan & Pearce, 1941), pp. 65-109.

[20]George Simon, *The Big Bands,* 4th ed. (New York: G. Schirmer, 1981), pp. 59-60.

[21]*Ibid.*

[22]MacDougald, "The Popular Music Industry," p. 69.

[23]*Variety,* 4 December 1935, pp. 37-38.

[24]Another, if not as meaningful, was the increased time given to news about the war in Europe, and the possibility of America's involvement in it, thus a smaller amount of time *available* for broadcasting music.

[25]MacDougald, "The Popular Music Industry," p. 109.

[26]*Variety,* 3 October 1945, p. 52.

[27]*Variety,* 25 June 1941, p. 36.

[28]*Variety,* 21 July 1948, p. 3.

[29]*Variety,* 9 April 1947, p. 39.

[30]The recordings, purchased at the nearby Liberty Music Store, were by Clyde McCoy and his orchestra.

[31]*Radio Broadcast* 5 (1927), p. 19.

[32]*Billboard Annual Supplement,* 27 December 1969, p. 58.

[33] From information supplied by the Music Publishers Protective Association in connection with and support of Senate Bill S590 (1955), dealing with revision of the jukebox exemption in the Copyright Act of 1909.

[34] *Variety*, 21 April 1954, p. 53.

[35] Lawrence W. Lichty and Malachi C. Topping, *American Broadcasting* (New York: Hastings House, 1975) pp. 439-40.

[36] Memorandum from Sidney M. Wattenberg, counsel for the Music Publishers Protective Association and the National Music Council, submitted in connection with and in support of Senate Bill S590 (1955), 7 March 1956, unpaged.

[37] *Variety*, 12 December 1956, p. 53.

[38] "Videola" enjoyed a short life that ended when the value of a performance was lowered by ASCAP and the television industry began to police its own operations by closer checks on programmers. The method was effective, but not nearly as dramatic as had been the British Broadcasting Corporation's action in 1948: when "pay-for-play" began to encroach on BBC programming, the Corporation not only barred the offending bandleader or artist from the air but also the entire catalogue of his collaborator (the publisher) for one year.

With the advent of television, *Your Hit Parade* went through the most important transition since its heyday in the 1930s. Television demanded something for the eye as well as the ear, and the program's staff responded by creating comic, dramatic, and romantic situations involving song-and-dance routines leading into the performance of each top song, now reduced from ten to seven. Plugs on television, as well as record and sheet-music sales, counted in the program's final listings. A song with "youth appeal"—*(They Try to Tell Us We're) Too Young*—made *Hit Parade* history in 1951, staying in the Number One spot for twelve weeks and on the show for a total of twenty-two. By 1958, however, production people had run out of ways to present popular music without "lip-synching" to recreate the highly individual performances that made new music popular. *Your Hit Parade* passed into history on 7 June 1958.

[39] Arnold Shaw, *The Rockin' '50s* (New York: Hawthorne Books, Inc., 1975), pp. 9-10.

[40] *Variety*, 16 May 1956, p. 55.

[41] Richard Schickel: "The Big Revolution in Records," *Look*, 15 April 1958, pp. 27-38.

[42] *The ABC of BMI* (New York: Broadcast Music, Inc. 1940), unpaged.

[43] Emanuel Celler on *The Barry Gray Show*, Radio Station WMCA, New York, 10 October 1956; and on *Between the Lines*, WABD-TV, New York, 30 September 1956.

[44] *Monopoly Problems in Regulated Industry*, Hearings Before the Antitrust Committee of the Committee of the Judiciary, 17 September 1956 (Washington, DC: Government Printing Office, 1957), pp. 4, 184.

[45] *Amendment to Communications Act of 1934*, Hearings Before the Subcommittee on Communications of the Committee on Interstate and Foreign Commerce, Senate Bill 2834 (Washington, DC: Government Printing Office, 1958), pp. 106-39.

While Vance Packard's "pallid, sullen young man" probably never knew it, in the previous year, Virgil Thomson, one of the plaintiffs who hired the expert on the "manipulation of American musical taste," had voiced a different judgment of Elvis Presley. Speaking at an American Round Table held at New York's Yale Club, Thomson remarked that " . . . a society must have some vulgarity if it is to have vigor and energy. As for Presley, his standard of professional operation is not low. He has never missed an engagement, or given a bad show, and that is the mark of a responsible workman. Twenty years ago, Frank Sinatra created a scandal as Presley does today. Frank Sinatra was at the time a first-class artist workman and so is Presley." (Quoted in *An Enquiry into the Social and Cultural Trends in America* [New York: American Advertising Council, 1957], p. 57.)

[46] Mike Gross, article in *Variety*, 8 January 1958, reprinted in *Amendment to Communications Act of 1934*, pp. 403-4.

[47] David T. MacFarland, "Up from Middle America: The Development of Top 40," in Lichty and Topping, *American Broadcasting*, p. 403.

[48] After the issue of damages was removed from the Songwriters of America lawsuit against BMI, there seemed to be little interest on most of the 33 plaintiffs' part to pursue the other charges. The case never came to trial and was dismissed with prejudice (thus precluding renewal of the complaint) and without payment of any costs by the defendants—none, that is, except the vast sums already expended on legal fees.

[49]*Statement of Paul Ackerman, Music Editor of The Billboard.* Printed for the use of the Special Committee on Legislative Oversight of the House Committee on Interstate and Foreign Commerce (Washington, DC: Government Printing Office, 1960).

[50]Bernard Schwartz: "The Real Payola," *New York Post*, 14 December 1959, p. 42.

[51]Among the defendants charged with illegal combination to monopolize music on radio and television was the Austin, Texas, broadcast property (and stockholder in BMI) headed by Mrs. Lyndon Johnson. It had been placed in trust for the Johnson family during the Texan's vice-presidency.

[52]Edward Eliscu, quoted in *Hearings on Copyright Law Revision in connection with H.R. 2223* (Washington, DC: Government Printing Office, 1975), p. 1,653.

[53]Lucia S. Schultz, "Performing-Right Societies in the United States," *Notes*, 35/3 (March 1979), 511-36.

[54]Testimony of Stanley M. Gortikov, quoted in *Hearings on Copyright Law Revision* (1975), p. 1,400.

[55]*Ibid.*, p. 1,568.

[56]Peter W. Bernstein, "The Record Business: Rocking into the Big-Money Beat," *Fortune*, 23 April 1979, p. 68.

[57]D. Duane Braun: *The Sociology and History of American Music and Dance* (Ann Arbor: Ann Arbor Publishers, 1969). Braun posits that 25% of the top hits came from Broadway shows in the 1929-30 period, falling to 15% in the next decade, and to between 5% to 15% during World War II. Movie and Broadway songs rose to 15% each annually after the war, but with the rise of rock-and-roll in 1956 each fell below 10% (actually 2.2% in 1958 and 3.3% the following year for songs from motion pictures).

[58]*Rolling Stone*, 18 February 1982, p. 49.

[59]Gortikov testimony, *Hearings on Copyright Law Revision* (1975), p. 1,395.

[60]Figures from *Billboard International Buyer's Guide 1978-79* (New York: Billboard Publications, Inc., 1980), p. 6.

[61]*Billboard*, 2 April 1982, p. 14.

[62]*Ibid.*, p. 1.

[63]*Billboard*, 2 October 1982, pp. 1, 15.

[64]Figures cited by Irwin Tarr of RCA Records, in "Tape Systems—Cartridge and Cassette: Current Impact in the United States—and Prospects," *The Complete Report of the First International Music Industry Conference, April 1969* (New York: Billboard Publishing Company, 1969), p. 251.

[65]*The New York Times*, 4 October 1982, pp. 1, C15.

The Institute for Studies in American Music at Brooklyn College, City University of New York, is a division of the College's Conservatory of Music. It was established in 1971. The Institute contributes to American-music studies in several ways. It publishes a series of monographs, a periodical newsletter, and special publications of various kinds. It serves as an information center and sponsors conferences and symposia dealing with all areas of American music including art music, popular music, and the music of oral tradition. The Institute also encourages and supports research by offering fellowships to distinguished scholars and, for assistance in funded projects, to junior scholars as well. The Institute supervises the series of music editions *Recent Researches in American Music* (published by A-R Editions, Inc.). I.S.A.M. activities also include presentation of concerts and lectures at Brooklyn College, for students, faculty, and the public.